Shrubs
Large *and* Small

Shrubs
Large *and* Small

Natives and Ornamentals
for Midwest Gardens

Moya L. Andrews & Gillian Harris

Illustrated by Gillian Harris

QUARRY BOOKS

AN IMPRINT OF INDIANA UNIVERSITY PRESS BLOOMINGTON & INDIANAPOLIS

This book is a publication of

Quarry Books
an imprint of
Indiana University Press
601 North Morton Street
Bloomington, Indiana
47404-3797 USA

iupress.indiana.edu

Telephone orders 800-842-6796
Fax orders 812-855-7931

This book is printed on acid-free paper.

Manufactured in China

See page 147 for Library of Congress
Cataloging-in-Publication data.

1 2 3 4 5 18 17 16 15 14 13

TO OUR PARENTS

Noel and Verne Landsberg (in memoriam)
Richard L. and Shirley Ann Donley Harris

Spicebush Swallowtail

Contents

List of Illustrations ix   Preface xi   Introduction 1

ONE . . . . *Shrubs Are Versatile* 7

TWO . . . . *Shrubs Attract Wildlife* 33

THREE . . *Bringing Flowers Indoors* 55

GALLERY 71

Appendixes 115   References 135   Zone Map 136–137   Index 139

Dried Hydrangea

Illustrations

1. Lindera   72
2. Amelanchier   74
3. Pieris   76
4. Viburnum   78
5. Chaenomeles   80
6. Aronia   82
7. Syringa   84
8. Cornus   86
9. Paeonia   90
10. Philadelphus   92
11. Physocarpus   94
12. Sumac   96
13. Itea   98
14. Calycanthus   100
15. Clethra   102
16. Vitex   104
17. Callicarpa   106
18. Hamamelis   108
19. Ilex   110
20. Evergreens   112

Each little flower that opens,
Each little bird that sings,
He made their glowing colors,
He made their tiny wings.

—*Anglican hymn,*
Mrs. Cecil Frances Alexander
(1818–1895)

Eastern Bluebird
and Staghorn Sumac

Preface

*T*he woody shrubs that we choose to grow, together with our trees, determine the architecture of our gardens. While we can easily change the herbaceous plants we grow from year to year, the shrubs are long-term residents and become a major part of the fabric not only of our gardens, but of our lives. For gardeners the passage of time is punctuated by what happens in the natural world around us and especially in our own little patch. Most of us enjoy the anticipation when a favorite shrub is in bud and about to bloom, or when it is time for special birds to appear in search of berries we provide in our shrub border. The expectation is often almost as satisfying as the reality.

The shrubs we select and grow near our homes, of course, reflect our priorities as well as our preferences. If we love flowers we choose as many deciduous flowering shrubs as we can. If we love the vibrancy of winged activity in our yards, we plant shrubs that provide food and shelter for birds and butterflies. We also plant some native shrubs to provide food for the caterpillars that will become butterflies and the other insects that are essential to the maintenance of our ecosystem. If we are concerned about the environment, we carefully avoid planting invasive species because birds eat their seeds and excrete them in the wild, where they (e.g., Asian honeysuckle, autumn olive, and other aggressors) can overwhelm our native plants. But most of us don't avoid including some benign imported plants that have proven to be good citizens in gardens here across many generations. These are some of our most-loved shrubs (e.g., lilacs and roses), which have lived on our shores since the days of the colonists. As well as having showy flowers, many of these traditional shrubs provide nectar for pollinators in the garden.

In this book we have showcased twenty of our favorite shrubs, and described many more garden-worthy varieties. Some are natives and some are imported from temperate regions in other parts of the world. The shrubs referred to as "natives" in this book are, but for a few exceptions, those that naturally occur in the eastern U.S., i.e., east of the Mississippi River and north of the Ohio, and Minnesota to Arkansas. Most are solidly Midwestern natives, and some are primarily denizens of the south that also venture north across the Ohio River. All are suitable for growing in the Midwestern garden. There are so many interesting and beautiful shrubs available that gardeners nowadays have no problem finding varieties that fit their needs and ones they will enjoy for years to come. Plant hybridizers have provided us with many new cultivars. Especially noteworthy are the small, slow-growing, and even dwarf shrubs that are now on the market. These make shrub maintenance so much easier, as older varieties often grew too big for small home gardens and required a lot of pruning to keep them in check. Now we can find a shrub for every site and one that is the perfect size at maturity if we read the plant tags carefully and do a little research before we make our selections.

One of the temptations for a modern gardener, faced with such a wide range of options, is to choose one of every shrub that is available, but we caution against having a garden made up of many singletons. Rather, one should choose three of a similar kind, or even five, if there is room. This usually helps to create an integrated design, though of course an occasional accent plant is useful, too. But a garden full only of accents usually ends up looking like a nursery.

We also urge gardeners to choose, as multiples and especially as accents, shrubs that have more than one season of interest. For example, while forsythia is gorgeous in spring, it has nothing to recommend it the rest of the year and the older varieties are hard to control. So we would certainly not want to have a front yard full of forsythia, as the interest is brief and the boredom is lengthy if such a bush is front and center. Rather, we suggest that a repertoire of shrubs of different types and with many varied seasonal attributes, such as foliage color and/or berries in fall, and branching structure and bark that are interesting in winter, be built up over time. For example, choose shrubs with bloom times that span different months and that provide a sequence of bloom so that the focus of attention moves around the garden at different times of the year. Of course, if a gardener has a nostalgic reason to grow a specific shrub, in spite of its providing interest in only one season of the year (e.g., "My grandmother grew it"), that is certainly a compelling enough reason to include it in the garden.

The best shrub plantings, from our perspective, are eclectic and include a number of our natives as well as some tried-and-true types of imported shrubs that have been proven to be well behaved and reliable in U.S. gardens. Such a mix includes specimens known to support native wildlife and to create a healthy and diverse ecosystem. After all, each sustainable home garden that exists is a microcosm of the macrocosm. It represents a step toward attaining the cumulative goal of restoring and protecting our nation's lands.

Shrubs
Large *and* Small

Introduction

The glory of gardening: hands in the dirt,
head in the sun, heart with nature.
To nurture a garden is to
feed not just the body, but the soul.

—*Alfred Austin*

For those of us who love flowers and want to grow masses of them, it is easy to lavish all of our attention on the annuals and perennials in our gardens and to ignore the shrubs. They stand there, large and small, so commonplace that we sometimes hardly see them, and yet they are essential elements of the architecture of our gardens.

A shrub is a woody plant with multiple stems. A close relative, the subshrub, has a woody base but top growth that is soft and that dies back after a hard freeze, just as herbaceous perennials do. A true shrub, however, has lots of woody growth arising from the base, unlike the single stem which is characteristic of a tree. This woody growth persists in winter after the foliage is gone and provides branching that adds charm to the landscape, especially when shadows are cast on snow. Some shrubs, like trees, have interesting bark as well. Birds and other wildlife appreciate the security of the cover provided by shrubs. The height of shrubs varies greatly: some hug the ground, and others grow as high as small trees, so height is not a factor in classifying a plant as a shrub. By definition, a shrub is a bushy woody plant with several permanent stems instead of a single trunk. Of course it is possible to train a shrub to have a single trunk, and when this is intentionally accomplished by human intervention, the plant that results is called a standard. Standards, because of the labor-intensive process involved, are always more expensive than shrubs with a natural shape.

Among the evergreen shrubs in gardens, there are those with leaves, such as the broadleaf rhododendron, and there are needle-bearing evergreens. Evergreens are essential in the winter landscape, and some, like holly with its fruit and rhododendron with its flowers, contribute color as well. Most evergreens, however, because of the mass and continuity of their basic color, contribute permanence to the year-round architecture of a garden and also provide useful backdrops for flowers in the growing season. Designers suggest that one-third of the plantings in a garden should be evergreen to carry the garden through the winter.

Many deciduous shrubs flower lavishly and become focal points in a garden when they bloom. So if a gardener chooses shrubs carefully, there can be a shrub in bloom at most times in the growing season. In autumn, color is provided by shrubs that have vibrant foliage and fruit. For example, *Callicarpa*, commonly called beautyberry, has yellow foliage and clusters of glistening purple drupes, and *Itea* 'Henry's Garnet' produces leaves that are mahogany red. It is characteristic of flowering shrubs to produce flowers low on their multiple stems, at eye level or below, unlike trees, where flowers appear at higher levels.

The shrubs in our gardens today are a mix of natives and those that were originally found by plant explorers in distant places of the world such as Japan, Korea, and China. Plant breeders have developed improved varieties of shrubs. Many old-fashioned, larger types of shrubs have been worked on by plant breeders so that now more compact varieties are available. This makes shrubs more available for use in small gardens and reduces the amount of pruning needed. Our grandparents did much more pruning of their lilacs and forsythias than we need to do today if we choose to plant smaller varieties of these old favorites. Additionally, old-fashioned shrubs such as althea, commonly known as rose of Sharon, are prolific self-sowers. If you planted one, you soon had hundreds. However, now there are sterile varieties such as the pristine white–flowering 'Diana' on the market, so we can enjoy these shrubs without having to remove unwanted seedlings. Shrubs, nowadays, if we select improved varieties of old favorites, need much less maintenance than they did in the past. When we examine the plant tags on shrubs before selecting which ones to buy, it is helpful to look for the Latin words *pumilus*, meaning dwarf or low-growing, and *humilis*, meaning shorter than typical, if we are shopping for compact varieties. *Grandis*, of course, means large, big, or showy.

Landscape roses are a category of shrub that has shown great improvement in recent years. The newer rose bushes are self-cleaning, do not need to be deadheaded to keep blooming, and are much more disease-resistant. Knock Out roses were the first introduction of low-maintenance roses of this type, but others have followed. Easy-care shrub roses are invaluable for color in the landscape. They are not a major topic in this book, however, since so much information is available elsewhere.

KNOW YOUR SITE

Gardening is an intriguing challenge as we try to coax our usually less than ideal plot to allow us to move closer to our dream garden. The way we site our plants is a major element contributing to both the overall design and the persistence and/or vigor of the plantings. It also affects flowering.

The longer we garden the more we understand the space, and we begin to understand why certain plants do better than others in the same location. For example, if you live in a region where spring often challenges you with a lot of freezing and thawing, place shrubs that you don't want to bud out too soon on the north side of your house, garage, or property. The shade cast by the buildings will help the shrubs to stay cold longer in spring and will keep them from budding out too soon and then getting zapped by a late freeze. Azaleas do well in a location like this, and some hydrangeas that bloom on old wood may benefit from such a site too. On the other hand, flowering quince and other very early bloomers such as witch-hazel (*Hamamalis vernalis*) may be better off if they are planted on the south or east side, where they get lots of early-season warmth and sunshine. You may have noticed that your earliest snow drops and daffodils love a southern exposure. Plant shrubs that like good drainage and hate having wet feet on slopes and in raised beds. Crape myrtles like this kind of location in full sun, and vitex also seems to enjoy it, as do the subshrubs. Notice flat areas or low areas in your yard where water stands longest after rain, and plant moisture-lovers such as buttonbush or silky dogwood in those places or by downspouts. When you find a shrub that thrives in a certain spot in your garden, add multiples of the same shrub and capitalize on your success. If everything you plant in a certain spot dies, carefully observe the wind, drainage, pattern of light and shade, and type of soil that exist in the trouble zone. Over time you will work out why it is a plant graveyard. A lot of gardening is trial and error and adaptation. A tree comes down in a storm, and what used to be a shaded area is suddenly in full sun. Or, conversely, a shrub that once did not shade its neighbors grows huge, and the neighbors can't compete. In such instances, pruning the shrub and/or moving some of the neighboring specimens might be necessary. One cannot emphasize too much the need for the gardener to consider carefully all of the conditions of a particular site and match the conditions with those on the plant tag. In the case of native shrubs, you can also observe them growing in the wild and take note of their habitats. Additionally, sites must continue to be monitored and assessed, so that corrective action can be taken, as groupings of plants mature and conditions change over the years.

Shrubs are forgiving plants and they are not high-maintenance. However, if they are not cared for at all, they will not reach their full potential. Besides, it seems that gardeners are by nature nurturing types, so they characteristically like to form relationships with their plants. Since shrubs are long-lived residents of a garden and their demands are minimal, it is usually satisfying to have shrubs in the yard.

Planting a Shrub

Giving the shrub a good start really pays dividends over time, and the bigger the hole and the more you amend the soil the better the start the fledgling shrub will get. Stand in your garden and look over the site you have chosen. Do the requirements on the plant's tag match what you have? Broadleaf evergreens, for example, need protection from the afternoon heat and winds, so a western exposure will not be ideal. Between 3 and 5 PM, the heat in summer can be extreme, so check if the site gets direct sun at that time if you are planning to plant a pieris or a rhododendron, for instance.

If the shrub's tag says full sun and lots of moisture, do not plant where the shrub's roots must compete with those of a tree, as the tree will suck up all the moisture, and the tree's canopy will reduce the amount of rain the shrub receives and will also produce shade. Under four hours of sun a day means the site is shady. Four to six hours a day means partial shade, and six or more hours constitutes a site with full sun. Check that whatever is growing near your proposed site (e.g., grass) is growing well and that there is space for the newcomer to expand and flex its branches as it grows.

Dig down about 5 inches to remove sod in a wide circle at least a foot and a half wide. Loosen the soil in the hole and mix in a bag of compost and vermiculite or organic matter (leaves, dried grass clippings, etc.) Dig down far enough in the loosened soil to bury the root ball. Remove the burlap covering of the root ball before planting and examine the root system. If roots have circled around tightly in the pot, or if they are broken, cut them off. Root pruning helps the plant get established in these instances. If you have a bare root plant, you must soak it in water, in the shade, for a few hours before planting it. Remember that the roots go upward, not downward, so the depth of the soil and its looseness and permeability are crucial for start-up feeding. The roots must get established first before top growth will begin.

Granular fertilizer, compost, or peat moss (especially for the acid-loving shrubs) should be worked into the soil as the shrub settles into the hole. The first new growth will occur at the ends of the roots, so splay them out so they lie horizontally. Then pour water into the hole to moisten everything well. Watch the water drain away as the goal is moist, not sodden, soil. Fill in and mulch heavily. If the site is on a slope, make a furrow so water does not run right off. If the site is on low ground, raise the area around the plant (plant it high) to improve future drainage.

Give the newly planted shrub a gallon or two of water a week for the first few weeks and for longer if the weather is hot and dry. The roots will be at the drip line (the edges of the branches) once the plant grows, so always irrigate well in a wide circumference around the trunk, as the feeder roots will be out from the trunk. Always keep a heavy mulch to conserve moisture, but keep the mulch from touching the tree trunk. Approximately 90 percent of the water will be used for cooling the plant, so broadleaf evergreens, such as pieris, that lose moisture through transpiration must be watched and watered carefully their first year as they are settling in. Acid lovers, such as blueberries, need regular application of acid (e.g., peat moss) as a mulch if they are grown in alkaline soil. Acid plant fertilizer and mulching with evergreen needles once a year also is helpful. Serviceberries, although adaptable to various soil types, appreciate some acid materials as a mulch too. They make good neighbors for evergreens in a mixed shrub border, with both evergreen and deciduous hollies, and *Fothergilla* 'Mt. Airy' (see appendix K).

ONE

Shrubs Are Versatile

No two gardens are the same.
No two days are the same in one garden.

—*Hugh Johnson*

hrubs, and for that matter all plants, are characterized by their form, their texture, and their color. Form and color change with time and seasons, and while texture may become more apparent as a plant grows, its defining attributes are usually consistent. The weight or mass of shrubs in a landscape is always greater than that of herbaceous perennials and annuals, but less than that of trees. The outline or silhouette is related to the shrub's form, but it will change with growth and also will be seen differently depending on the perspective from which it is viewed. The light conditions and the amount of obstruction presented by neighboring hardscape and buildings, as well as other plants, will also contribute to the way a shrub's silhouette is perceived by a viewer. At different times of day shadows will also be cast by garden shrubbery, and every shrub will, of course, be seen differently in various seasons. In winter when there is snow cover, the silhouette of a deciduous shrub will be quite different from the one the shrub presents with its summer or fall foliage intact.

Trees and shrubs provide the most solid masses in garden design and are the elements that either frame and enhance the houses in residential gardens, or partially obscure them from view. Shrubs are used to mark boundaries, screen eyesores, and delineate areas within garden spaces. In residential gardens the scale of plantings and the way the woody plants are grouped are crucial to the harmony of the landscape. The woody plants are the elements that provide the architectural structure. In both the creation of vistas and the development of enclosures, woody plants play a starring role.

When choosing the correct site, a gardener must think about the size each particular shrub will attain at maturity in order to ensure that the scale of plantings will be right. If adding a new shrub to an existing landscape, a gardener must consider how a new addition will blend in or contrast with existing plantings. If we are selecting a deciduous shrub that loses its leaves in winter, we might consider how the shape and branching will look in relation to existing plantings in the cold months, as well as how the foliage color and texture will look during the growing seasons. If the plant blooms, we need to think about what else will be in bloom at the same time, in order to ensure harmony in terms of color across the landscape. When in doubt about this aspect of the selection process, always choose a shrub with white flowers.

In cold climates, a garden should contain about one-third evergreen and two-thirds deciduous plantings. Evergreens come in a variety of colors, sizes, shapes, and textures. Their foliage can be broad-leaved, as in rhododendrons, small-leaved, as in boxwoods, or needle-shaped, as in spruces and hemlocks. Their shape can be large or small, rounded or cylindrical, upright or spreading. Their textures can be spiky, as in hollies, wispy, as in pines, or dense, as in yews. Their colors can be various shades of green, blue, gray, or yellow.

Evergreens can be lined up like soldiers to form a perimeter planting, or used alone to provide accents. They can be massed together in blocks for convenience—e.g., on a bank or slope that is hard to mow. They can be placed strategically across a large landscape in order to provide repetition. In formal gardens, clipped evergreens provide patterns and organization for spaces. They may be used to line paths, to outline small areas or beds, or to fill urns. They are used to provide the balance and symmetry that are essential characteristics of formal designs. In informal gardens evergreens can also help organize separate areas by providing year-round hedges. Hedges can be high or low, depending on whether they are to be screens, and can be straight, curved, or serpentine in formation.

The size of a garden will determine how much space can be allocated to mass plantings of evergreens, but there should always be some to provide winter interest and shelter for wildlife. If a gardener is also a flower arranger, the winter garden should include some evergreens that yield materials that can be cut for indoor arrangements.

The type of conditions the plant will need to adjust to is an important consideration when a gardener is choosing both evergreen and deciduous shrubs for a landscape. If native plants are sited appropriately, they usually settle in without much pampering, so it is helpful to become familiar with native shrubs and their habitats in the region where we live. Natives are usually more susceptible to our pests and diseases than cultivated imported varieties from other continents that have temperate climates like ours. However, they frequently tolerate local weather conditions better than nonnatives. Additionally, the presence of native plants in our home landscapes helps to alleviate the loss of wild shrubs to development, providing food, shelter, and nesting places for wildlife.

UNUSUAL SHRUBS

Most gardeners love well-known shrubs such as lilacs and roses, which have been brought here from overseas. Some have been here since colonial times and are much loved. However, we also have lots of unusual native shrubs that we are gradually learning more about and that we could use more than we currently do in our home gardens. Think about the native witch-hazels, for example. *Hamamelis virginiana* (autumn-blooming witch-hazel) grows the largest, and although it is multi-stemmed like a shrub, if left to its own devices in a woodland setting it can grow to 30 feet. It has a distinctive vase-like shape and is in full bloom in October and November. It is hardy to zone 3. Ozark witch-hazel, *Hamamelis vernalis*, is hardy to zone 4 and has a late winter/early spring bloom near the vernal equinox. Its flowers are about three-quarters of an inch across and are yellowish to orange-red. Autumn foliage is yellow and provides a special bonus.

Japanese plum yew (*Cephalotaxus harringtonia*) is hardy to zone 5 and grows tall in sun or shade in well-drained soil. It makes a valuable hedge or can be used as an accent. Since deer savor yew foliage, gardeners in deer-populated areas may like to layer more deer-resistant plants in front of yews. For example, in a shrub border, place the yews against a wall or garage to form a hedge. Then, in front, place a line of the deer-resistant *Abelia mosanensis*, which has fragrant pink flowers May/June and good fall color. Another deer-resistant shrub such as fiveleaf aralia (*Eleutherococcus sieboldiamus* 'Variegatus'), hardy to zone 5, and with yellow May/June flowers and handsome variegated foliage, could be selected for this layer. The native buttonbush (*Cephalanthus occidentalis*, see appendix G), hardy to zone 4 with globe-shaped white flowers in July, followed by reddish balls of seeds, grows in sun or part shade and is also an underused native shrub that is deer-resistant.

Gardeners who are looking for plants for heavy shade might like to try the Japanese aucuba, which is hardy to zone 6 with protection. It is an evergreen and produces red fruit. The oakleaf hydrangea (*H. quercifolia*) and native wild hydrangea (*H. arborescens*) will also bloom in shade, as will the native spicebush (*L. benzoin*), which as a bonus is deer-resistant. *Kerria japonica* will bear yellow blooms from June to September in sun or shade if the soil is moisture retentive. Variegated kerrias are available, and they provide foliage interest in woodland settings. An interesting evergreen that grows in shade is a dwarf Japanese cedar (*Cryptomeria japonica* 'Knaptonensis'). White new growth changes to lime green in zones 6–9 and it grows only 2 feet tall with an 18-inch spread, so it is a good edging plant.

Forsythia is a nuisance shrub after its spring display, as it spreads and needs a lot of pruning in return for only one season of pleasure for its gardener. If you want to grow it plant a dwarf such as *F. × intermedia*, which grows only 18 inches tall and 30 inches wide.

Deutzia scabra 'Codsall Pink' is a good accent plant with double pink blooms in May, reaching a height of 6–10 feet in zones 5–8 in a sunny, well-drained spot. An added attraction is the exfoliating bark and bare branches that arch gracefully and are useful in winter flower arrangements. Another sometimes underused shrub for accents is the smoke bush (*Cotinus*), which now comes in a variety that has golden foliage all season in zones 5–8 and attains a height of 10–15 feet. It can be cut back to make it a smaller bush and can be combined with the traditional smoke bush with purple foliage in sun or part sun, in berms, borders, and avenues. Don't overlook our native *Viburnum acerifolium*, which has purple foliage in the fall and black fruit, making it a good accent plant, too. It grows in dappled shade and can be combined in a large grouping—at the edge of a wooded area, for example, with cutleaf maple (*Acer japonicum* 'Dissectum'), star magnolia (*Magnolia stellata*), and *Hydrangea paniculata* 'Grandiflora' or other hydrangeas. However, if you have deer problems, substitute *Viburnum nudum* 'Winterthur', a native cultivar that has white flowers June/July, wonderful fall color, red berries, and most importantly, deer resistance. It grows 5 feet by 6 feet in zones 5–8.

Now that the USDA has updated the Plant Hardiness Zone Map due to the warming trend of the past few decades, most of us experiment with some shrubs that used not to be recommended for our area (visit www.arborday.org /media/mapchanges.cfm for an animated map showing the changing zones). Our options with respect to shrubs we can consider planting are greater now than they were previously. Also there are many underutilized natives, as we will be discussing in subsequent sections of this book, that can enrich the diversity of our home garden shrubbery.

TAKING STOCK OF OUR PROPERTY

Whether the property where we garden is new to us or we have gardened on it for years, we generally can benefit from carefully evaluating its assets and liabilities. Is it currently a densely populated space or is it a blank slate? How many trees are there? How many shrubs? Are there existing beds, and if so are they in appropriate locations? Are there any valuable or favorite plantings we wish to retain or move? What are the sunny and shady sides of the house? Where does the sun rise and set and what shadows are cast at noontime? What is the ratio of wooded areas to open areas? What kind of soil is there? What plantings adjoin the garden perimeters and what does the region contribute in terms of wildlife to attract? Is there a deer problem?

Shrubs that like good drainage and dislike wet feet will enjoy a sloping site more than shrubs that require even moisture. An example of a subshrub that thrives on slopes and in raised beds is lavender, which originated in the Mediterranean region. Remember that subshrubs have a woody base like shrubs, but soft top growth like perennials. Never cut into the base of a subshrub when pruning. Another excellent choice for a dry (and even rocky) slope is the low-growing native shrub New Jersey tea (*Ceanothus americanus*). Shrubs such as hydrangeas that do not tolerate drought well should not be planted on slopes or in raised beds. Site them in low spots or near drainage ditches or downspouts.

The exposure of the site is also a key factor in the placement of new shrubs in a garden. Generally speaking, azaleas and rhododendrons, which do not grow exuberantly in the Midwest, prefer the north side of a house or other structure. Since the north gets less winter sun than other exposures, these shrubs will not break their dormancy as early on the north side as they would, for example, on the south side, and are therefore less vulnerable to freezing and thawing as well as to the cold winds that dry out their foliage.

Set Some Goals

Once we have taken stock of our existing property and/or plantings, we are in a better position to decide on both long-term and short-term goals. When you embark on a rejuvenation of an existing garden, consult with experts to learn the names of your existing plants, trees, and shrubs and discover which shrubs are exotic (and perhaps undesirable invasives) and which are natives.

Waiting and observing a newly purchased garden for a year, before ripping any plants out, is usually judicious too, as a new owner then sees what the landscape looks like in all seasons.

Most of us tend to concentrate on spring and summer plantings, but a garden should be attractive in fall and winter as well. The birds also appreciate both food and shelter in those seasons of the year. Think about shrubs with interesting bark and branching structure that will be good for you to look at and for the birds to find shelter in during the coldest months. Remember, too, that we always need both vistas and enclosures in our gardens and try to maximize opportunities to capitalize on both of these by using shrubs that are attractive across the entire year.

HEDGES

Hedges, made up of similar individual shrubs, have been important features of European gardens since records have been kept. A low hedge was a popular way to enclose medieval herb gardens, when herbs were grown for medicinal purposes. Parterres are ornamental gardens where flowers and foliage are grown to form patterns, and they were often viewed from high windows overlooking courtyards of stately homes in Britain and France in centuries past. Knot gardens and parterres, as well as cloister gardens, usually had small edging plants that were trimmed to maintain specific heights and widths, and so were extremely high-maintenance. Since World War I, however, when maintaining labor-intensive gardens on large European estates became impossible for most families, we have seen fewer examples of trimmed hedges, except in public gardens. Low boxwood hedges are seen sometimes edging beds of herbs and roses and along paths in formal gardens. Higher clipped evergreen hedges are also still used in some modern formal gardens where spaces are enclosed to form garden "rooms," or where paths lined with evergreens lead the eye toward a focal point, or distant vista.

Not all hedges are alike, however. The Romans used box, laurel, and myrtle in hedges in the gardens of their villas, and tall holly and cypress hedges are still seen in some Italian villa gardens that are open to the public in our century. In some English country gardens today we can still see gardens with trimmed yew hedges forming a lush background for flowerbeds. Sometimes hedges are trimmed so that they frame statues, entrances, and benches within enclosed garden spaces. Hedges like these evoke a sense of permanence and anchor plantings within the enclosure they provide. Of course hedges of similar evergreens, carefully maintained, are the essential ingredient in mazes, which provide some of the most challenging and most unusual arrangements of evergreen plantings and involve structure, order, and repetition as well as ingenuity in their design.

Shrubs for hedges as well as other types of plantings are available in many sizes and can be evergreen or deciduous. They contribute height and mass to a garden, and if they are chosen and placed carefully, they can provide not only a feeling of permanence but also a succession of interest across all four seasons. While shrubs are not as high-maintenance as annuals or perennials, they do require some attention in order to remain attractive year-round. Since shrubs are long-term residents of a garden, it is best to spend some time on the selection process and on decisions regarding their location. If one is starting a new garden from scratch it is wise to develop a landscape plan, with careful personal research, or in collaboration with a professional designer.

We now know that privet is an invasive species and so do not advise using it for hedges. Boxwood is a better choice. However, privet hedges are sometimes seen in older gardens and many appear overgrown, with all of the foliage on top and lanky leafless legs beneath. This is because the top portion of the hedge has become so wide that the lower limbs do not get much sun. Hedges like this can be renewed if they are cut back and then gradually shaped so that the top portion is narrow enough that sunlight can penetrate and leaves can grow on the lower limbs. The ideal shape for a mature hedge is to have the base several inches wider than the top, and sides that slope gradually inwards from bottom to top. Always allow plenty of space on either side when you plant a line of shrubs to form a hedge lining a path. The plants must be permitted to grow a little each year to remain vigorous over time, so although trimming will be done, all hedges have a tendency to end up taking up more space than the gardener imagines they will at first. Evergreen hedges are ideal for enclosures for secret gardens and private tranquil spaces. Their advantage is that their impact remains across four seasons.

Pruning

Living hedges form walls in gardens and range in height from 1 foot to large trees. As well as being trimmed and trained in various ways, they can also be left to grow as nature intended and to arch and billow as their growth patterns dictate. Untrimmed hedges at first require no special care, although eventually they need to be checked lest they outgrow their space. In order to train a hedge, however, it is often necessary to cut back the annual growth by about half until the desired height (and/or width) occurs. This process helps create denser branching. Formal hedges consisting of evergreen plants such as arborvitae, hemlock, yew, and box should be clipped annually. Privet, which grows quickly, may need multiple clippings each year during the growing season. Deciduous as well as evergreen shrubs can also form low-maintenance hedges if dwarf shrubs are used.

Choice of Materials

Gardeners can choose any shrubs, evergreen or deciduous, to form a hedge. One can mix and match in balance and combinations too. However, to perform well in a hedge planting a shrub should be capable of producing even growth, should put out thick branches and foliage close to the ground as well as higher up, and should have relatively small, textured leaves that withstand frequent trimming. Deer love evergreens such as arborvitae and yew but do not seem as interested in spruce or boxwood. Check local nurseries to find deer-resistant plants if Bambi frequents your garden.

Installation of Hedges

The site must be especially well prepared and carefully measured so that the line of shrubs when planted is straight and not crooked. If the shrubs are to be planted in a semicircle or spiral, serpentine or zigzag pattern, the measurements will need to be even more exact than if the hedge is to be a straight line. Sometimes a double row of shrubs may be used. Before planting, it may help to use stakes with string attached or a garden hose to delineate the outline to be followed. Since plants will be closer together in a hedge than in any other grouping of shrubs, there will need to be good light and air circulation and extra good nutrition in the soil so that the plants can grow together in a healthy fashion even though their root systems are crowded. Do not plant hedges along walls or under trees, as these will compromise evenness of growth and vigor. Lilacs and non-native viburnums are heavy feeders, so they are not good neighbors in hedges bordering flowerbeds, as their roots will infiltrate the space under the borders. For hedges near flowerbeds, select box, arborvitae, or juniper as these shrubs have roots that will not range out more than about 3 feet.

SHRUB BORDERS

Shrub borders are often planted at least two shrubs abreast. Borders usually back up to a fence or wall or other design element that allows them to be

Glossy leaves, fragrant pink flowers	*Abelia* × *grandiflora* (glossy abelia)	Zone 6	Height 5–6'	Do not trim
Red fall foliage	*Abelia mosanensis*	Zones 4–6	Height 5–6'	Do not trim
Purple flowers	Combine *Abelia* with *Vitex*	Zones 5–9	Height 4–5'	
	Acanthopanax sieboldianus (fiveleaf aralia)	Zone 4	Can be clipped or left to grow 7–9'	
Deep blue flowers, green foliage	*Caryopteris* (bluebeard or blue mist spirea)	Zones 5–8	*Caryopteris* 'Dark Night' 30"	
Dense foliage, dark purple flowers	*Caryopteris* (see app. F) 'First Choice'		Height 2–3'	
Gold foliage, amethyst-blue flower spikes	*Caryopteris* 'Sunshine Blue'		Height 2–3'	
White spring flowers, lime yellow foliage	Combine with *Deutzia* 'Chardonnay Pearls' *Deutzia gracilis*	Zones 5–8	Height 2–3'	
	Deutzia scabra 'Codsall Pink'		Height 6–10'	
White spring flowers, blue/green foliage, colorful in fall	*Spiraea* × *media* 'Snow Storm'		Height 3–4'	

EVERGREEN

Pyramid-shaped with deep green waxy leaves (male)	*Ilex* ('Blue Boy'), zones 5–8
Ilex × *meservae*	'Castle Wall', height 5–8'
Ilex × *meservae*	'Castle Spire', plant 3' apart
Tsuga spp. (hemlock) N.B. The hemlock woolly adelgid is a major threat to hemlock trees that has now spread to the Midwest through nursery stock.	Grow in dry shade in Zones 5–8
Taxus cuspidata and *T.* × *media* cultivars	

viewed mainly from the front. Usually a taller shrub is at the back, and often this is evergreen if the border is used as a screen. Shrubs that will have flowers, or that will require more attention, deadheading, or pruning, are usually placed toward the front of a shrub border. Often ground-hugging shrubs will be placed at the edge of a border (e.g., 'Blue Star' juniper) to form a living mulch which keeps both watering and weeding to a minimum. Pruning is often minimal in a carefully planned shrub border if dwarf varieties are used and deadheading is not needed.

Deciduous shrubs can produce flowers either on old growth made the previous season, or on the current season's new growth. For example, kerrias, forsythias, weigelas, and old-fashioned hydrangeas carry their flower buds in their old canes. This kind of shrub does best when the canes are pruned back immediately after they bloom. It gives the bush ample time to develop new shoots. When the flowers are produced on the current season's growth, the flowers usually appear later in summer/fall on spring growth. This type of shrub is best pruned in late winter, or in colder climes, when all possibility of frost is over. Dead or thick older growth is taken off back to the main trunk. Shrubs such as hardy hibiscus, abutilon, crape myrtle, smoke bush, and vitex are in this category, as well as the white flowering hydrangea 'Annabelle'.

It is possible to have a long sequence of bloom, fall color and berries, and winter interest in a shrub border if shrub material is carefully selected. Shrubs make an impact in a garden because they can be situated to create a mass that provides an architectural presence. The most solid living mass in all seasons is provided by evergreen shrubs, and these are generally chosen for foundation plantings and hedges and may be shaped and clipped to varying degrees. Holly, hemlock, Japanese yew, and English boxwood can be pruned well for these purposes.

Topiary: This involves pruning evergreen shrubs into figures and playful or formal shapes that are quite removed from the natural shape of any plant. Topiary was first seen in Roman gardens. Japanese yew, hemlock, English boxwood, and holly are typically selected for topiary plantings today.

Espalier: Deciduous as well as evergreen shrubs can be trained and pruned to grow into atypical forms. When shrubs and small tress are trained to grow branches that are horizontally flat against a brick wall or wooden fence, the method is described as *espalier*. This process involves the pliable limbs of shrubs being trained to grow at right angles to their trunks, with the branches fastened to wires or nails. Yews (*Taxus* spp.), *Cotoneaster horizontalis*, *Pyracantha* spp., and fruit trees are frequently used.

Thus, sometimes the height, width, and form of shrubs are tightly controlled, as in formal clipped hedges, and topiary and espalier, while at other times shrubs of varied sizes, forms, and colors are encouraged to grow naturally or in less-regimented ways. However, care must always be taken to plant shrubs with the correct *spacing* between specimens so that, as they grow and mature, either they grow together uniformly, or they can attain a desired growth, with or without pruning, to form a pleasing composition with a variety of natural forms.

FOUNDATION PLANTINGS

In *mixed foundation plantings,* a variety of shrub heights (low, medium, and tall) may be used. Usually the shorter shrubs will be placed in front of windows so that views are not obstructed. Taller specimens will be placed at the ends or corners of buildings. Some shrubs may be pruned and others left to grow to form natural and/or irregular shapes. The whole composition, however, should be balanced—not necessarily exactly symmetrical, but with equality of mass, substance, and height on either side of the front door of the home. The plants should also be set far enough forward that there is adequate air circulation between the house and the back of the shrub. For more formal plantings, evergreen shrubs may be pruned to create cushions, spires, or cones that are compatible with the architecture of the building. Urns containing small evergreens are sometimes positioned to flank entrances or paths.

Paths to the front door of a home should always be wide enough to accommodate two persons walking abreast. An entrance path's surface should always be constructed of safe materials for people to tread on, and appropriate lighting should be provided. Sometimes paths are curved from curb to door if there is enough distance between the street and the entrance. When the path is straight it may be softened with free-form low plantings that flank it or rows of clipped edging composed of plants such as lavender, boxwood, or prostrate creeping evergreens such as junipers. The colors used in the hardscape and the plantings should harmonize at all times during the growing seasons, especially when annuals or perennials supplement the shrubs.

Scale is also a consideration when foundation plantings are selected. For example, the size of shrubs at maturity must not be too overwhelming for the height of a low, one-story ranch home. A two-story home may be able to accommodate taller shrubs, or even small trees on the corners and sides of the house, as long as they are placed so that windows are not obstructed. A large house and yard will not look as attractive in terms of scale if there are only a few small shrubs dotted in the front of it. Conversely, huge unpruned shrubs and trees, when they are mature, will overshadow a small house and cause it to appear even smaller than it actually is.

Color is also an important variable with regard to foundation plantings. Evergreens may be selected in shades of green, gray, and yellow. They can also be selected to have berries for winter interest. The colors selected should harmonize with the colors of the home and the hardscape, as well as the urns and planters that contain both evergreens and summer annuals or perennials. For example, a home with a red roof and/or red trim may not be the best background for a tub of red petunias or geraniums, as reds are often hard shades to mix and match.

Shape is important, not only in the items that make up the foundation plantings but also in the items that are used in urns and planters around a home. For example, in patio tree-form shrubs, pompom, spiral, and poodle topiary shapes would not be compatible if just one of each different kind of topiary was selected. Rather, repetition of shapes, with those in urns and those in the ground reflecting similar forms but different sizes, would be more appropriate in a formal setting. In a more naturalistic garden landscape, repetition of similar forms, such as fountains of grasses of different sizes and colors, would complement a more rustic informal foundation planting on a residential lot.

The principles of composition to follow in any grouping of shrubs are related to the amount of similarity and dissimilarity of size, form, shape, texture, and color. Also, the number of items that repeat key characteristics, versus those items that present contrastive characteristics, must be considered carefully in order to create balance and harmony.

A *large mass* of identical evergreen shrubs will certainly anchor a foundation to its site if all the individual plants exhibit similar outlines, color, and texture. The similarities will give a lot of weight to a massed planting. However, over time, if the shrubs are not pruned they may grow so large that the home may seem to be engulfed by them. Eventually, the architectural details of the home could be completely obscured by greenery. Yet the role of foundation plantings is to soften the site, especially the base of the walls of the house, and to enhance rather than to engulf. Rather than just thinking about the foundation plants, the landscaper should consider the whole gestalt of the home and garden—i.e., the back and sides as well as the foreground. The front plantings should always include some variation in the shrubs, but not so much as to distract from the overall harmony of the entire home and landscape. Harmony is achieved by having more similarities than differences in form. Interest is added by a few (but not a lot of) contrasting forms and/or elements. A sense of order and coherence is created by having a number of similar forms with just a few contrasts to provide some interest to the composition.

While it may seem to be a good idea to include a mass of similar evergreens, some different shrubs should always be added for accent, or to contrast with the predominant color of the evergreens and thereby provide some variation in mass and weight. For example, if the predominant evergreens are yews, a few low-growing blue spruces could be added for color, and would add contrast in form and texture too. To add more variation in texture, two *Pieris japonica* shrubs could be added as accents, as these shrubs also bloom. It is wise to resist the impulse to add a large number of different shrubs to the mix, as too many disparate shrubs in a small evergreen planting can create a sense of disorganization rather than harmony. One way of imagining patterns in evergreen shrub groupings is to think of musical notes, with just one note being significantly higher or lower than the other notes in a phrase. A shrub pattern, like a musical pattern, can be put down on paper during the planning phase.

TIPS FOR FOUNDATION PLANTINGS

· Keep it simple. Choose only three species to include in a small-to-medium-sized area, but select three plants from each species for repetition. In a large area use five items from five different species to create unity, and they will demand only a minimum of care.
· Replace any overgrown existing shrubs if there is already a foundation planting. When removing them saw the trunks off at the base if possible. Leave the roots in place until they die a bit. You may need professional help to extract large root systems. You may, however, be able to plant new small shrubs between the old root systems, which will gradually decay with time.
· Dwarf varieties of shrubs have become available in greater numbers in recent years. It makes sense to plant dwarfs, as constant pruning is the only other way to keep bushes small. See appendix C.
· Before there were many dwarf shrubs available in the trade it was usual to allow shrubs to grow to a height that reached to the bottom of the windows of the house. However, the lower the shrubs, the larger the house will look. It is only the foundation of the house that needs to be obstructed from view, so choose low-growing shrubs for new or renovated planting. Then add vertical interest with carefully placed flowering shrubs as accents. If the masonry of the foundation needs it, paint it to either match or contrast with the color of the home before you plant the new shrubs. The color could match the front door and window shutters, for instance. It could also be a darker shade of the color of the paint of the house.

- Place shrubs several feet away from the house so that there is air circulation and shrubs get maximum light. Mulch the area behind the shrubs so that mud does not splash onto the house when it rains. Mulch the entire area so that weeds are discouraged. Mulch usually contains a seed germination deterrent. A layer of weed barrier fabric under the organic mulch suffocates weeds that try to grow from seeds already in the soil when the planting is done. Hand pull or judiciously use herbicides for persistent weeds that poke through.
- If the foundation planting adjoins lawn, put in an edging or mowing strip as an alternative to having to trim. Wood edgings are not advised, as grass grows between them, whereas a flat brick strip allows the mower wheel to straddle it when the edging line is mowed.
- When pruning shrubs, always place a tarp or sheet under the shrub to collect the clippings. Then gather the corners and drag the clippings to the compost heap. Always use sharp pruning shears that are well oiled, or use electric hedge clippers. Wear gloves, especially for prickly bushes like hollies. If grasses are in the planting, tie string securely around the base and middle and top of the clump. Use a tarp so that the grass bundles fall onto it as you make cuts under the string. Otherwise pieces of grass will fly in all directions and will be difficult to rake up.
- Boxwoods can be a variety of shapes, including columnar for vertical interest. They like well-drained soil, so put them away from downspouts and set them in a wide hole at the same height they were in their pot. They have shallow roots; do not disturb them by planting annuals around them. Dwarf cultivars need no pruning. Larger ones should be pruned in late spring and again in midsummer. Do not prune in the fall as it stimulates new growth, which can then be damaged by freezing winter temperatures.
- In zones 4–7 or with protection, *Cotoneaster* species are shrubs that can manage less-than-optimal conditions such as seaside plantings in sun or shade, and they can survive dry winds and droughts. They come in a variety of shapes and sizes and require little attention once established. They have small white/pink flowers in spring and summer, followed by red or orange fruits which are savored by sparrows, robins, bluebirds, cedar waxwings, and birds that nest in the larger varieties of these shrubs. There are different cultivars depending on the characteristics that are needed: creeping, fruiting, leaf color, ground coverage, etc. They all have

shallow root systems, so they need ample water until established and then are maintenance-free except for the removal of dead wood.

- Do not plant burning bush (*Euonymus alatus,* or winged euonymus) in foundation plantings—or anywhere else, for that matter, as it is an extremely invasive species. Choose alternative groundcovers such as creeping evergreen junipers, which are cold-tolerant and low-maintenance, or other deciduous shrubs that present a large selection of upright shapes and sizes. Plant several together and consider foliage in dark green or golden chartreuse (full sun brings out the color) or gray- or blue-green. Mature width may exceed mature height, so place carefully and consult plant tags. Low-growers are good for slopes, and verticals are best for punctuation accents. In cold climates plant in early spring to ensure they are well rooted by winter. Water well the first year.

- *Liriope* (*L. muscari* and *L. spicata*) and plumbago (*Ceratostigma plumbaginoides*) are ideal to install as groundcovers edging shrub borders or around foundation shrubs. Because it appears in late spring, plumbago can be planted with daffodils to hide their decaying foliage. It has lovely little blue flowers in summer and red foliage in fall. In zones 5–9 it likes a mix of sun and shade. In tropical areas there is a light blue (*Plumbago auriculata*) that is drought-tolerant. *Liriope,* hardy to zones 5–10, is a good edging and also groundcover in shade or sun. It shrugs off humidity and drought, it has either blue or white flower spires, and some varieties have variegated leaves. Ask for the kind that spreads by stolons if you want groundcover. Do not use that type as an edging, however, as it will grow out of bounds.

- Serviceberry shrubs or small trees can be planted at the corner of foundation plantings. These deciduous natives have delicate white flowers in spring, red fruit in summer, and bright fall foliage. Their lovely gray bark and attractive branching are revealed in winter. Serviceberries are pleasing in naturalistic shrub plantings, in woodland areas, and near ponds. There are many native varieties to choose from, as well as the cultivars *Amelanchier* 'Prince Charles' (good fruit), 'Princess Diana' (disease-resistant), and 'Autumn Brilliance'. Hardy to zone 3, they are very adaptable, but they grow best in full sun. They like moist, well-drained acid soil best, so combine them with evergreens in mixed shrub borders, as the needles will provide some acidity for them.

Mass plantings are always seen from more than one vantage point, and individual shrubs are usually planted in more than one row or are staggered. Shrubs, unless they are planted as sentinels or to line an avenue, are rarely planted in regimented straight lines, though this may occur in groupings where there is layering. When shrubs are layered, it is best, of course, to plant the shortest shrubs in front and the medium ones behind the shortest, with the tallest in the back. If the shrubs outgrow the height that the gardener wants, then corrective pruning is needed on a regular basis. In a garden where different layers of shrubs will be blooming at different seasons, or times of the year, the pruner must be especially vigilant in order for the succession of blooms to be seen to advantage. See appendix A for a summary of which flowering deciduous shrubs should be pruned.

Island Beds

If shrubs are in an *island bed*, the tallest shrubs will be like a mountain range in the middle of an island. The medium-height shrubs will be planted around them, and the shortest shrubs will serve as a perimeter edging for the bed. However, variations are infinite.

Dwarf spireas (see appendix E) that are excellent re-bloomers can be obtained, and many have the added bonus of foliage color (chartreuse). Weigelas have also been vastly improved by modern plant breeders. Foliage variations are now available as well as repeat bloom in many cultivars. This shrub is also a magnet for hummingbirds and grows in zones 4–8. *Vitex* produces sprays of blue/purple flowers in summer and has handsome, fresh-looking foliage.

Berms

Berms are island beds that have had additional soil and organic material added to them so that the area is like a free-form raised bed. When a garden has drainage problems (e.g., a low, boggy site, or a sloped site which experiences runoff during rain), a berm is an excellent location for a shrub planting. If screening is needed by a homeowner (e.g., a barrier planting on a property adjoining a busy street), a berm is an excellent solution, as the height of the shrubs will be increased markedly by their having their roots in the raised soil that makes up the berm. Many gardeners lay out the outline of their berm with a hose so that size and shape in relation to the entire property can be decided on, through trial and error, the fall before the shrubs are to be planted the following spring. Then autumn leaves are raked to build up the site, as well as other organic materials such as newspapers and cardboard sheets, grass clippings, peat, and manure. The site then sits as the materials break down all winter, and it is ready for plants the next spring. This process is sometimes referred to as lasagna bed preparation. Some berms are created to be large enough to include small trees. As trees grow, however, they will cast shadows on the other plants in the berm. The gardener can deal with this eventuality by planting shade-tolerant shrubs, of course, though the available shade will be minimal during the early stages of a tree's growth. Suffice to say that if trees are included in a berm, the exposure and amount of shade cast on other plantings will need to be carefully considered.

Our examples of shrubs that combine well will not include any trees. Tall shrubs are suggested instead to provide the height needed in a berm used for screening. If screening across the year is the most critical function of a berm planting, then the majority, if not all, of the shrubs should be evergreens of some type. Choose varieties that will thrive under the conditions in the spot chosen. Few shrubs will do well in full shade (no sunlight), but full sun is not always desirable for some evergreens either. Read the plant tags and assess the type of light available as well as the kind of soil in the area. By planting shrubs that like the conditions you have, you are likely to be successful. The broadleaf evergreens such as rhododendrons, azaleas, boxwood, holly, and daphne have different requirements from the narrow needleleaf evergreens. Evergreens come in a variety of sizes and shapes such as round, prostrate, compact, open, and weeping. Some produce cones and berries, and some have special pruning needs (e.g., spruces will not regenerate if the growing tips at the ends of their branches are cut off). All plants that are purchased should have root balls that seem adequate in terms of the top growth, and there should be signs of top growth. Make sure that the plant tag specifies the soil, light, and water needed by the variety of plant that you are purchasing. Also check the zone to match the plant's needs. It will need more protection if it is not listed as hardy in a zone a bit colder than the one where it will be planted. As a general rule dwarf evergreens are best for small gardens, as are slow-growing varieties that will not get too big too quickly. For example, littleleaf cotoneaster (C. *microphyllus*) is a good slow-grower for semi-shade.

BROADLEAF EVERGREENS

Rhododendrons, azaleas, mountain laurel, holly, pieris, and sourwood dislike strong sun and winds in winter and too much heat in summer and thus need plentiful moisture year-round. They must have acid, well-drained soil. They flourish in woodland settings and next to north or east walls. They also like not to have to compete with tree roots. Amend the soil well if the garden soil is clay. Try to add sand, compost, and acid peat, and fertilize early each summer with an acid fertilizer. Mulch with oak leaves or pine needles. Do not let these plants dry out in summer or winter. Spray with an antidesiccant in late fall to prevent leaves dehydrating because the plant loses water into the atmosphere at too high a rate in cold weather. Spray with deer and rabbit repellants also.

A berm that combines both broadleaf and needleleaf evergreens would probably do best bordering a woodland area. The selection of deer-resistant evergreens would be an important consideration, however. Some gardeners who suffer from too many deer suggest liberal use of herbaceous peonies as edging plants, since deer usually leave them alone. They also spray regularly with deer deterrents.

MIXED SHRUBS FOR BERMS

Berms that are planted with both evergreen and deciduous shrubs can exhibit changing accents and focal points across the seasons. The first blooms in late winter appear on the late-winter-blooming witch-hazels. Vita Sackville-West loved the Chinese *Hamamelis mollis* and the Japanese *Hamamelis japonica* 'Arborea' because the Asiatics have early flowers that last a long time and scent a whole room. The native *H. vernalis* also blooms in late winter to early spring. Cultivars include 'Carnea' (pink flowers), 'Red Imp' (red petals with orange tips), and 'Squib' (vivid yellow flowers). Viburnum and daphne 'Somerset' (*Daphne* × *burkwoodii*) shrubs are fragrant spring bloomers also, so these are deciduous shrubs to consider as well as the early-blooming flowering almond bush, lilac, and ninebark. Smoke bush is quite dramatic in the summer landscape, with dark foliage and smoke-like tresses of bloom. Early fall accents can be obtained by planting crape myrtle, caryopteris, and callicarpa, with its lustrous purple fruit clusters. Shrubby species of dogwood are also good options. In windy sites, Harry Lauder's Walking Stick (*Corylus contorta*) provides a wonderfully twisted form both when in leaf and when bare.

Plant mounded shrubs as well as tall columnar evergreens like yews and boxwood. Contrast these with deciduous winterberry hollies, which have spiky branches with large red drupes that show up so well in the fall. Remember to plant both male and female holly plants in order to get fruit. A large mixed evergreen and deciduous planting must be carefully planned. The repetition of different forms, colors, and shapes helps provide an organized rather than haphazard effect. For shrubs to include in mixed plantings on shaded berms, which can present more of a challenge, see appendixes I and J.

BANKS AND WALLS IN SUN

Sometimes there are sloping areas in gardens that are very difficult to mow. One solution for dealing with such an area is to shore it up with a wall or make a raised bed out of timber. Another option is to plant shrubs close together on the slope so that grass and weeds will not grow. The area around the shrubs can be heavily mulched, and weed barrier fabric can be placed under the mulch. On top of walls, a layer of shrubs can be planted. First, edge the ground with a creeping plant that will in time droop over the top of the wall and soften it. This can be a perennial such as creeping phlox that blooms in spring, or a subshrub such as candytuft or lavender, both of which will enjoy the excellent drainage. Behind this first layer, plant a line of dwarf perovskias, because a Russian sage will also enjoy the heat reflected from the wall and the good drainage. Behind these first two layers could be planted a number of different flowering deciduous shrubs depending on the gardener's preferences concerning the height, type, and color of bloom and the desired bloom time. If a tall layer of shrubs would be appropriate to the area, a plant with dark foliage such as *Sambucus nigra* 'Black Lace' would offer a striking contrast to the gray leaves of the perovskia in front of it. A sterile variety of rose of Sharon, such as 'Diana', which will not self-seed, could be used also. Lilacs are another option. If a shorter shrub is desired, the old-fashioned spring bloomer pearlbush (*Exochorda*, often sold under the trademarked term *Snow Day*) could serve well. It blooms May to June and attains a height of 3–5 feet. Creeping needle evergreens can also be used to drape over and soften the walls.

Slopes

If there is a large sloping area to be covered, large spreading evergreen or deciduous shrubs should be considered. Large spreading evergreens or the deciduous bottlebrush buckeye, *Aesculus parviflora*, will grow in sun or part shade.

This buckeye (see appendix S) grows into spreading mound-shapes reaching 8 feet tall with a spread of 10–15 feet. It produces spectacular erect spires of white blooms in July. It prefers moist, slightly acidic soil. A smaller shrub that is also useful for a mass planting on slopes is flowering quince. New varieties have been developed, such as *Chaenomeles speciosa* 'Toyo Nishiki', which grows 4–6 feet high and spreads 4–6 feet wide in about five years. The spring flowers are lovely and look beautiful in flower arrangements, and the branches can be forced. Bees and hummingbirds love them. Yellow fruit is produced in the fall. The fruits can be used for jelly and are aromatic, as a bowl scents an entire room. This shrub blooms best in full sun and any soil that is well drained. Since it produces suckers, it makes a good spreader on a hillside. It must be pruned in winter and the dead wood removed, but be sure to cut back only about one-quarter of the stems each year so that bloom is not sacrificed. In hot, dry sites, deciduous beach plum (*Prunus maritima*), broom (*Cytisus* spp.), and shrub honey locust (*Gleditsia triacanthos* 'Elegantissima') can also be used.

Shrub Maintenance

Shrubs are low-maintenance plants, but they do need some care. They are not as high-maintenance as perennials because they do not need as much deadheading or cutting-back; however, some of them must be pruned periodically or they will become overgrown and unsightly and provide few blooms. If a gardener likes to prune or has a family member willing to do so, a shrub garden is not difficult to maintain. The rules about pruning are simple, and nowadays it is easy to look up information on the Web. However, most flowering shrubs should be pruned right after they bloom on old wood or on branches formed the year before. There are some shrubs that bloom on new wood, i.e., new growth. Those plants, especially the ones that bloom in later summer or fall, can be pruned in late winter or early spring and still have time to grow the new wood which produces the flowers later in the growing season.

Remember, no haircuts—i.e., straight-across pruning, as it destroys the natural shape of the shrub. (See appendix A.) Instead, selectively cut out the thicker branches right to the base of the shrub. The thinner canes are the newer canes, and those produce the most flowers. If plants sucker and spread from the base, these shoots should be removed when they appear. If a shrub is badly neglected and needs to be completely rejuvenated, it is fine to cut it right to the ground; however, it may mean that the shrub will not put out any blossoms for a year or so while it grows back. Some fertilizer once a year and watering during periods of drought are also wise strategies. Always water new plantings well for the first season to help their roots get established in the new location.

Hydrangeas like a lot of water, and when a gardener plants a new one it is imperative that the information about it is carefully considered. Older types all bloomed on old wood, whereas the new varieties that are being developed bloom on both old and new wood. Once it was the rule of the gardeners in the Midwest that the white-flowered hydrangeas that bloomed in late summer, such as 'Annabelle' (*H. arborescens*), were the only ones that bloomed well. This was because in areas where there is frequent freezing and thawing in spring, the new buds in the old canes suffered terribly—resulting in few, if any, blue or pink blooms most years. Since the white varieties bloom on new wood later in the summer they were the only reliable bloomers in areas with fickle spring weather. Check your hydrangeas carefully and ask the garden center when you purchase them about their blooming type and time and when they should be pruned. Remember that deer do eat every type of hydrangea and that hydrangeas need moisture and prefer some shade. *Hydrangea quercifolia* 'Snow Queen' is an improved form of oakleaf hydrangea that is more upright and compact.

Dwarf evergreens have been developed in a variety of colors and forms in recent years, and this makes it easier for gardeners who have space constraints. It is also convenient to have dwarfs and/or very slow-growing varieties because it eliminates a lot of pruning. The definition of *dwarf* is an evergreen that is under 8 feet tall ten years after it was planted. Most dwarfs only grow about an inch a year, so it is a long time before they outgrow a space. Generally speaking, conifers do not like wet feet, and some, including the *Tsuga* (hemlock) varieties, will grow in shade and will even tolerate dry shade once established. All conifers provide wonderful year-round texture in a garden. In areas that often get very wet spring weather, plant them where the drainage is good (slopes, raised beds, berms) so their feet never stand in water. Seek out dwarf shrubs with colors and shapes that meld well with companion plantings and home exteriors. See appendixes C and H for suggested varieties. *Picea glauca* 'Pixie Dust' has yellow growing tips on the ends of the branches, and *Pinus contorta* 'Spaan's Dwarf' thrives in hot, dry spots. For exceptionally hot and dry areas of your yard, use cypress varieties. Combine these shrubs with native perennials that tolerate drought well because of their taproots: *Echinacea, Asclepias* (butterfly weed), and *Penstemon* species.

Plants are adaptable, but they are more likely to flourish if we pay attention to their basic needs. Few plants will grow in constantly wet soil, so drainage is always a concern. If plants are on a slope or in a raised bed, they will have dry feet most of the time. Plants that enjoy dry conditions, including the subshrubs, lavender, Russian sage, rosemary, and culinary sage, thrive in these locations. If you are seeking companion plants for your shrubs in a well-drained berm, for example, choose from the following list of perennials that bloom early.

Plants That Enjoy Sharp Drainage

Creeping phlox (*Phlox subulata*) grows in full sun and flowers in April/May in pink, white, and lavender shades. Use it as an edging to drape over walls or slopes. It is evergreen to zone 3 and likes hot sun. Shear it back after it flowers. The lavender-colored varieties seem the most vigorous.

Pinks (*Dianthus* spp.) are also good edging plants for dry sites. They have pink flowers and various combinations of pink, white, and burgundy, and they start blooming in May with some repeat-blooming. Gray spiky foliage remains all year in zone 3.

Catmint (*Nepeta* spp.) produces blue flower spires in late spring and re-blooms if the gray foliage is cut back. It has aromatic foliage, which usually deters the deer, and it likes full sun. Choose a low-growing variety for the foreground of shrub plantings.

Culinary sage (*Salvia officinalis*), which has gray leaves and is a subshrub, has blue/purple flower spikes in May, grows 1–2 feet in full sun, and is hardy to zone 4. It is a fairly short-lived perennial but worth replacing every 3–4 years. The ones with variegated foliage are the most short-lived in our Midwestern gardens.

Late Bloomers

If you are looking for companions for shrubs planted in sites with good/excessive drainage and need plants that will bloom late in the growing season to combine with the shrubs, try the following perennials:

Mallow (*Malva fastigiata*) tolerates dry soil conditions and is hardy to zone 3. It has flowers dotted along the stems in mainly white, pink, and lavender shades. It flowers consistently from June to frost and reaches a height of 2–3 feet. It does not need deadheading, but the deer eat it, which is a major drawback. *Malva sylvestris* 'Zebrina' is a bicolor with appealing burgundy veining and attractive foliage.

Hummingbird hyssop (*Agastache rupestris*) is a subshrub that is aromatic, so deer don't seek it out. It grows 1–2 feet in sun to zone 3 and is attractive to hummingbirds. It starts blooming in July and continues till frost.

Moisture Lovers

If you are wanting plants to grow in a moist area of your garden—near downspouts, for example, or at the bottom of slopes where water pools and is slow to drain, try some of the following as companions for shrubs that enjoy moisture-retentive soil:

Rose mallow (*Hibiscus moscheutos*) is often called swamp mallow, as wet feet do not cause problems for this plant. It grows 3–7 feet tall, produces white or pink flowers in July/August, and is hardy to zone 4.

Golden alder (*Alnus incana* 'Aurea') likes wet sites in sun.

Ironweed varieties (*Vernonia fasciculata* and *V. gigantea*, which is the tallest at 5–8 feet) produce purple flowers in July/August and like sun and [either[wet or dry soil.

Joe-Pye weed (*Eupatorium fistulosum*) grows 4–7 feet and produces clusters of small pink flowers in July/August. Shorter varieties can be obtained. It likes full sun in moist to wet soil.

Marsh blazing star (*Liatris spicata*) grows 2–4 feet and sends up purple flower spikes with rounded tops in June/July. It is hardy to zone 3 and likes sun to part sun and moist to wet soil.

Beebalm (*Monarda didyma*) grows 2–4 feet, produces shaggy blossoms in red, white, magenta, and lavender shades in June, and is hardy to zone 3. As a member of the mint family, it is a vigorous spreader in moist to wet soils and sun to light shade. It is aromatic, so the deer do not devour it, but I have seen them eat it. However, it is susceptible to powdery mildew. It is useful as a cut flower in informal arrangements. To slow down its vigorous spread, it can be easily pulled up, so selectively edit the clumps when picking the blossoms. Another strategy is to plant this moisture-loving plant in a dry part of the garden so that it does not have optimal conditions for its needs and does not spread as much as a result. It attracts hummingbirds.

Swamp milkweed (*Asclepias incarnata*) likes full sun and wet soil but must be deadheaded to continue blooming after it starts in late June. It grows 3–4 feet and even taller with good moisture, and produces pink flower heads. It is hardy to zone 4.

Meadowsweet (*Filipendula purpurea*, and also *F. palmata* and *F. ulmaria*) varieties love moist to wet soil in sunny spots and are hardy to zone 3. They grow to between 2 and 5 feet and may reseed if there is no seed germination deterrent in the mulch used around them. They all produce pink or white fluffy-looking flower heads in May/June. Pick the flowers before the florets are fully open and keep plenty of water in the vase if using them as cut flowers.

Plants for Wet Shade

Goatsbeard (*Aruncus dioicus*) is a shrubby native perennial that will grow as large (3–6 feet) as a bona fide shrub if given the conditions it likes. It prefers partial or dappled shade, with protection from hot afternoon sun, and likes rich, evenly moist soil. It grows in zones 3–7. In full bloom it makes a handsome specimen, with feathery clusters of creamy-colored short and thin flower spires. The attractive green foliage sets off the elegant flower display from early summer to midsummer. There is also the shorter (8–12 inches) *A. aethusifolius*, which could look at home by a downspout in a foundation planting or as a low hedge at the base of a slope where it gets the necessary consistent moisture to thrive.

Turtlehead (*Chelone glabra*) produces white flowers and is a native wildflower, growing 1–3 feet tall, that likes rich, moist soil and full sun. The blooms are tubular, with two lips that appear from late summer to fall. *C. lyonii* is pink and hardy to zones 3–8 and will grow in part shade and full sun, as will *C. obliqua*, which has rose-purple flowers and also likes moisture but is only hardy to zones 5–9.

Cardinal flower (*Lobelia cardinalis*), blue lobelia (*L. siphilitica*), and forget-me-not (*Myosotis palustris*), as well as native ferns such as royal fern (*Osmunda regalis*), cinnamon fern (*Osmundastrum cinnamomeum*), and various sedges (*Carex bromoides* and *C. nigra*) also enjoy sites in wet shade. Zones 5–9.

Rose of Sharon is a fall-blooming shrub that enjoys moisture. All types that are sterile (such as 'Blue Bird') are recommended, as they will not self-sow.

Other members of this mallow family like moisture too, as well as some shade, and they extend the season of bloom. Zones 4–7.

Ligularia has spikes of flowers in late summer and handsome large leaves all season. *Ligularia dentata* 'Britt-Marie Crawford' has chocolate foliage and orange flower spikes. Shade to part shade with consistent moisture; zones 4–7.

Native *Arisaemas* Jack-in-the-pulpit (*A. triphyllum*) and green dragon (*A. dracontium*) also like well-drained but moist shade in zones 5–9.

TWO

Shrubs Attract Wildlife

Bees and blueberries must make their pollen
deal in May if robins and blueberries
are to make their seed deals in July.

—Sara Stein

Use plants to bring life.
—*Douglas Wilson*

L ike trees, most shrubs are long-lived. However, they mature faster, and in four years or so after planting, they will flower and/or fruit well. When we increase the number and variety of shrubs we grow, our garden becomes more diverse and is better equipped to attract different types of birds, who depend on a diversity of habitats for food, nesting spots, and shelter. Shelter involves having a safe place in which to minimize the effects of excessive wind, sun, rain, snow, and hail. A garden also needs to provide hiding places that screen birds from their predators. For example, predators that pounce on their prey from above cannot see through dense evergreens.

Evergreens, especially dense ones such as yews and spruces and large-leaved rhododendrons, provide excellent cover for mammals and birds during heavy snows and downpours of rain. They also serve as protective roost sites for juncos and other birds in winter. In the summer, deciduous shrubs provide shade from the hot sun. Protection from strong winds is also provided by hedges and hedgerows, and mourning doves and other birds that roost at night in a flock often can be found sheltering in shrubs and trees that form windbreaks. Cardinals and mockingbirds like to nest in shrubs with branching that provides a secure site for their nests. In winter we can see and take note of the deciduous shrubs that birds nested in the previous spring and summer. Diversified planting encourages both migrants and breeding birds to frequent our gardens.

Shrubs attract insects for birds to feast on and provide nectar-rich flowers, seeds, and fleshy fruits to eat. The bright color of fruits and their position on the ends of branches make them highly visible to birds, who while enjoying the fruit sugars also ingest the seeds. They later excrete the seeds, most likely in another location, and thereby aid the shrub in its seed dissemination (this can be a problem when the shrub is an unwanted invasive species).

It is advantageous, if one wants to have lots of birds visit, to think about planting shrubs that fruit, and/or produce their flowers, at different times of the year. In the spring, serviceberry, chokeberry, flowering almond, flowering quince, and lilac produce flowers. Weigela, buddleia, and hardy hybrid hibiscus such as 'Southern Belle' are useful for summer flowers. Virginia witch-hazel blooms in autumn. Serviceberries fruit in late spring, blueberries and raspberries in midsummer, and viburnums, elderberries, and dogwoods in late summer or fall. Beautyberry, with clusters of iridescent magenta drupes, is a must-have fall-fruiting shrub. Ilex species, both the evergreen holly and the deciduous winterberry holly, retain drupes for birds to eat in the colder months, but remember that there must be a male plant nearby for female hollies to produce fruit.

Shrubs are woody plants that usually grow between 3 and 15 feet tall. They are low-maintenance except for when they are first planted and need regular watering while they get their roots established. In times of drought, and especially if shrubs are planted in a raised bed or on a sloping site, check that they get the moisture they need. Usually the drooping or dryness of the leaves signals lack of water. Since shrubs are usually more expensive than herbaceous perennials and annuals, it is wise to water them deeply at least once a week the first season after they are planted and thereafter weekly during hot, dry spells.

Pruning out dead wood and old, thick canes keeps shrubs rejuvenated. As a rule, deciduous shrubs are pruned immediately after blooming has finished. This is because some shrubs bloom on old wood and others on new wood, and so it is safest to prune before the possibility that new buds may be set. However, shrubs that bloom on new wood, including buddleia, crape myrtle (see appendix L), and amsonia, can be cut to the ground in late fall or very early spring as only the new growth the next spring will produce the blossoms.

Useful shrubs to place near bird feeders are junipers, rhododendrons, yews, spireas, sumacs, roses, and hollies. If feeders are placed near the window of a home, plant shrubs to enclose the feeders and birds will use them for shelter and protection as well as for nesting. This is equivalent to humans living next door to a grocery store or cafeteria (just be sure that house cats can't pounce on the birds from nearby shrubs). Summer fruit-bearing bushes such as serviceberries, blueberries, blackberries, and gooseberries can be combined with alders and dogwoods on the edge of woods or as screens to attract birds on larger properties. In small gardens, planting decisions must of necessity be strategic. New Jersey tea and aromatic sumac are two natives whose smaller size makes them suitable for gardens with limited space. Plant breeders have also produced many dwarf versions of flowering and fruiting shrubs, and these provide wonderful opportunities for gardeners with small plots to have diverse plantings that do not require much pruning to maintain a manageable size and shape. Dwarf shrubs also give gardeners the opportunity to avoid having a whole yard full of different single plant specimens. A group of three or five of the same type always is preferable to just one of a kind. Five viburnums, for example, could be planted in a serpentine hedge to protect bird feeders placed in an angle formed by two walls of a house.

Repetition is an essential element in design, and repeating shrubs of the same form, height, and texture helps to anchor and integrate a landscape. For example, as a screen between neighboring houses, a tall row of columnar evergreens such as arborvitae or the holly *Ilex crenata* 'Sky Pencil' could be flanked by a row of deciduous mid-size flowering shrubs such as *Viburnum plicatum* 'Summer Snowflake'. Alternatively, for the row of deciduous shrubs, *Sambucus* (elderberry) could be used, as its dark foliage contrasts well with the evergreens. For example, *S. nigra* 'Black Lace' has dark, deeply cut, ferny-looking leaves. Small pink flowers in summer are followed by black fruits. If space permits, a third row of dwarf flowering quince, *Chaenomelis* × *superba* 'Cameo', would provide early spring bloom. When fruiting shrubs are planted it is especially helpful to plant multiples of each variety, rather than just one specimen of each. The more fruit available, the greater the number and variety of birds drawn in. More leaves also attract insect larvae that provide valuable protein for the birds, especially when they are nesting, feeding their young, or migrating.

The branching of the shrubs must be strong enough to support a nest but not too dense. Thorns can inhibit nest-building, so thornless shrubs seem to be the most comfortable for birds going in and out of their nests, though some birds do build in large rose bushes. Lone shrub specimens in open areas do not seem as likely to have birds nest in them as do groups of shrubs or shrubs planted near trees and flowers. This is because insects can be found in the crevices of the bark of adjacent trees, and nectar and seeds are available from nearby blossoms and grasses.

Hedgerows

A *hedgerow* is, by definition, a long line of shrubs and/or small trees at the edge of a lawn or a field. Hedgerows may be planted in any sunny spot to divide areas of a large garden or to mark boundaries. They require some maintenance over time, as volunteer trees and weeds will grow up and undesirable species (e.g., the ubiquitous Tree of Heaven) will need to be removed. However, willows, serviceberry, elderberry, viburnum, ninebark, American beautyberry, rose of Sharon, dogwood, sumac, alder, lilac, yew, sage, and even mock orange and spirea can be incorporated to provide diversity and a succession of flower and foliage interest. Spicebush has both flowers and fruit and is a larval plant for the spicebush swallowtail butterfly, so it is an excellent choice.

Highbush cranberry is a native viburnum, with white flowers followed by red glossy drupes in late summer that appeal to birds such as the lovely cedar waxwing. Viburnums in general are an excellent source of food for birds, as are serviceberries and dogwoods, and shrubs of the *Rubus* genus (blackberries). American hazelnuts (*Corylus americana*) are fine, thick bushes that can grow up to 10 feet high. They are adaptable to a variety of soil types and spread by stolons to create natural hedges. Try grouping them along the edge of woods; as long as they receive sun, they will produce nuts. Wild hazelnuts are smaller than the commercially grown kind, but are still tasty if one can harvest them before the wildlife does. They are a favorite of squirrels, as well as turkeys, woodpeckers, bluejays, and pheasants. In the colder months, the male catkins are a food source for ruffed grouse and woodcock.

Flowers can bloom sequentially across the three growing seasons in a garden that has a varied planting of shrubs. The trick is to choose carefully so that some shrubs are always in bloom. Include some evergreens in deciduous hedgerows for extra wildlife cover in winter. Some evergreen shrubs that can be combined with deciduous ones in areas that are sunny are *Juniperus* species (juniper berries are also an important food source), *Abies koreana* 'Aurea' (fir), and *Picea glauca* 'Jean's Dilly' (spruce). For partially shaded sites try *Taxus canadensis* (our native yew), *Buxus sempervirens* 'Vardar Valley' (boxwood), *Chamaecyparis obtusa* 'Fernspray Gold' (false cypress), or *Cryptomeria japonica*

'Knaptonensis'. Do not rake the leaves around a hedgerow, as insects, toads, and salamanders may shelter beneath them. Some gardeners put dog hair from their pets, needles from pine trees, dry grass, and other materials useful for nest-building near to their shrubs and hedgerows each spring. Putting out nest-building materials for birds is something adults can encourage young children to do with them. Since not enough seeds are typically produced in a home garden, the provision of sunflower seeds (hulled and black oil if possible), mixed seed, and thistle seed in feeders is also important for attracting birds. Setting out suet, and peanuts or peanut butter, will bring in woodpeckers. Involve children in this activity, too, and they will learn more about the interdependence of different species.

Teach the children in your life about the different varieties of birds that come to your garden and how they, and migrating birds that pass through, need water as well as food and shelter. Moving water that makes the slightest trickling noise is especially effective at drawing in wildlife. Make sure all of your water features are safe for young children to be around and encourage them to fill shallow saucers with water from a watering can so that birds can drink and bathe. A bird feeder is a wonderful gift for a young child, just as a pair of binoculars may be an interesting gift for an older child. But of course the gift of your time and the sharing of your fascination with the world of nature is by far the most precious gift of all.

FLOWERS AND THEIR FUNCTION

What Leslie Woodruff did to his lilies is no different from what
a bee or a butterfly would do: he brushed pollen from the
stamen of one flower onto the stigma of another.

—*Amy Stewart, writing about the man who developed the 'Stargazer' lily*

We do not know exactly what the first flowers on earth looked like, but their process of evolution into the flowers that we see today has taken millions of years. However, flowers acquired many of the characteristics that endear them to us (e.g., color, scent, and shape) as a means of attracting pollinators. Their purpose is reproduction. Each plant has to make sure that its species survives, and so flowers have evolved in many different ways. Plants' survival is dependent upon the production of seeds, and flowers play the starring role in reproduction. Most flowers are bisexual, but they can also be exclusively male or female. Remember how we have to plant male as well as female holly plants, for example, in order to have holly berries?

THE REPRODUCTIVE STRUCTURES OF FLOWERS

The male organs in flowers are the stamens that produce male cells (pollen). The pollen grains develop inside the anther, which is part of the stamen. The female sexual organ is the pistil, which produces female cells (ovules) inside an ovary. Only one tiny grain of pollen is needed to fertilize an ovule. The grain attaches to the stigma on the pistil and sends a pollen tube down into the ovary. After fertilization the ovule develops into a seed and the ovary into the fruit surrounding the seed.

The grains of pollen adhere to the stigma of the flower's pistil because it is sticky. However, pollination won't occur in all cases. Only pollen from the same or a closely related species usually results in successful pollination. When the pollen comes from the stamens of the same flower or the same plant, self-pollination occurs. If the pollen comes from the flower of a related species, it is referred to as cross-pollination.

In modern times humans have become actively involved in plant pollination, and this has resulted in human engineering of cross-pollination. This occurs in order to breed characteristics that are desirable, such as vigor and disease-resistance in plants and brighter colors and different forms of flowers.

HYBRIDS

New plants produced through cross-pollination are called hybrid plants, and if hybrids self-seed in our gardens the flowers of the offspring are not exactly the same as those of the hybrid parent-plant. This discrepancy also occurs with foliage characteristics. When we write the name of a hybrid plant we use a multiplication symbol to indicate the cross between the two parents. For example, *Cytisus* × *praecox* 'Hollandia' is an early-blooming hybrid broom. In Latin, *praecox* means premature, and 'Hollandia' is a cultivar (cultivated variety), so single quotation marks are used around that name. If we were referring to a naturally occurring species of the genus we would capitalize the genus and not capitalize the species (e.g., *Cytisus multiflorus*), and there would be no multiplication symbol.

Cytisus × *praecox* 'Hollandia' is a compact woody shrub that is a quick grower in zones 5–9. It withstands drought once established. It is a good shrub for flower arrangers as it has arching branches bearing fragrant, pea-like salmon pink flowers that are excellent for cutting and that hold up well in a vase. Broom is a native of the Mediterranean regions and when grown outdoors prefers sunny sites. The flowers are sometimes forced indoors and the less hardy species may be grown in greenhouses in colder climates.

HOW POLLEN IS TRANSPORTED

Natural cross-pollination between plants has contributed to the gradual evolution of most species over time. Changes will occur when two plants of the same species, that may have slightly different characteristics, combine. If a new characteristic is a helpful one for the plants, it tends to persist and may even be exaggerated in the successive generations if it directly benefits the plants' adaptation and survival. To increase the odds of cross-pollination within the species some flowers are sterile to their own pollen and to the pollen from plants of other species.

Agents

Self-pollination is the least complicated method to transport pollen, as the pollen just falls onto the stigma of the same, or an adjacent, blossom. However, the wind is a very common way for pollen to get dispersed further afield, and tree and grass pollen travels far this way—causing much discomfort to humans who are allergic to it. It is a lighter pollen than that produced by the flowers of plants and shrubs in our gardens. The earliest flowers on earth were probably wind-pollinated. Only a few plants transport their pollen by floating it on the water, but some aquatic species do it this way. Many flowering plants, though, rely on animals, and animal pollination occurs when animals are attracted to plants because of some benefit to themselves. Insects are the most frequent visitors to flowers, though a few small rodents and bats visit, and of course some birds, such as hummingbirds, are lured by the nectar.

Plants use the energy from sunlight and their own chlorophyll to form carbohydrates from water and carbon dioxide, and the process is called photosynthesis. Animals cannot do this conversion, so they must seek out sources of food from plants. During the millions of years of evolution both the flowers and their visitors seeking sustenance have adapted themselves to each other.

While ants walk to flowers, the vast majority of visitors fly to plants seeking the food they offer: pollen, nectar, seeds, fruit, and leaves. Nectar is a watery solution of sugars, produced by some plants for the sole purpose of attracting visitors, mainly insect visitors. A few flowers do not produce any nectar at all, relying instead on extra pollen as their special attraction. The best transporters of pollen from flower to flower are the flying insects such as gnats, flies, wasps, bees, beetles, moths, and butterflies.

The most prized pollinators attracted to the garden may be hummingbirds and butterflies—indeed, we create entire gardens specifically for these captivating creatures.

The most efficient and effective pollinators, however, are those insects, such as the bees, whose larvae depend entirely on pollen collected by the adults. Hummingbirds and hummingbird moths hover while feeding, and butterflies prefer to perch atop an inflorescence while daintily sipping nectar through their long proboscises. Thus the amount of pollen picked up by them is relatively small. Butterflies and moths drink nectar only as adults; in their caterpillar stage they feed on leaves. Bees, on the other hand, must collect enough nectar and pollen to feed themselves and their larvae, and to create enough honey to see the hive through the winter. They feed often and heavily, and as they crawl over and inside blossoms to reach the nectar with their short tongues, they pick up pollen on their hairy bodies, and readily distribute it as they fly from bloom to bloom. Thus bees are the superstars of pollinators.

Honeybees

There are many bees native to North America, including the familiar bumblebee. The honeybee, *Apis mellifera*, perhaps the best-known plant pollinator, has been resident in the western hemisphere for only about four to five hundred years, since Europeans brought hives to America. Honeybees' relatively large, stable social colonies and efficiency in converting pollen to honey has made them the key pollinator in commercial agriculture. The process is nevertheless quite labor-intensive for the bee; on average a hive of honeybees fly about 55,000 miles and visit approximately 2 million flowers to produce one pound of honey. At the same time they pollinate vegetables, fruit and nut trees, and a myriad of other plants on which our agricultural economy relies, including those consumed by meat and dairy animals. In California, beehives are transported by truck to orchards and fields and released to pollinate the plants. After one crop is pollinated, and the bees have returned to their hives, they are moved on to the next crop. All told, about one-third of the food we eat is made possible by the honeybee. For this reason the recent phenomenon of "colony collapse disorder," in which bee colonies go into sudden, steep decline (now thought to be the result of a combination of disease pathogens, environmental factors, pesticides, and other stressors) has alarming ramifications for food production worldwide.

Bumblebees

Bumblebees, members of the genus *Bombus*, are also social insects, but their colonies are typically much smaller than the honeybee's, and most species do not overwinter. The bumblebee is larger and "furrier" than the honeybee, and its thick hair enables it to remain active in colder weather, making it an important pollinator in more northerly climates. The bumblebee's pile also works to a flower's advantage. As the bee flies, its branched hairs actually build up an electrostatic charge that attracts pollen to it when the bee lands on a flower (which is firmly grounded to the earth). When the bee visits the next bloom, the stigma, being the most solidly grounded part of the flower, pulls this pollen dust off the bee's charged hairs, and fertilization takes place. Thus the bumblebee, while gathering food in the baskets on its legs, inadvertently transfers pollen from one flower to another.

The fascinating symbiotic relationship between plants and pollinators is vital for life on our planet. By choosing a variety of flowering shrubs for our gardens that are attractive to pollinators, throughout the growing season, we are contributing to a healthy ecosystem. Moreover, there is no more delightful place to be than in a garden full of bright, fragrant blooms, vibrant butterflies, and the hum of working bees.

Metamorphosis

Some insects go through metamorphosis, or the transition from larvae to adult, gradually; except for size, they don't exhibit significant differences in their appearance during the progressive stages of their life cycle. They eat similar food at all stages of their lives. Other insects differ greatly in their larval and adult forms, and they frequently have different dietary requirements at each stage. For instance, the caterpillars of both butterflies and moths eat leaves, while the adults eat nectar. Therefore, if a gardener plants shrubs with flowers to provide nectar as a way of attracting butterflies, but then uses pesticides to spray the bushes because caterpillars are eating holes in the leaves, the gardener's efforts to have a garden full of butterflies will be doomed to failure. It is necessary to sacrifice some leaves to nourish the caterpillars in order to have the adult butterflies.

Beneficial Insects

Gardens with a diverse array of plants, including a significant representation of natives, and the avoidance of invasive species and pesticides, create a healthy and inviting habitat not only for pollinators, but also for beneficial insects. As many an organic vegetable gardener knows, beneficials act as gardener-assistants when they are welcomed into the landscape, offering free services such as aid in controlling pests and improving the soil. A source of water in a garden can be a magnet for beneficials. It need not be an elaborate water feature, as just a clay saucer filled with pebbles and refilled daily with water will suffice. Damselflies and dragonflies need water for their young nymphs. They, like praying mantises, eat flies, mosquitoes, and aphids. Ladybird beetles, whose larvae resemble tiny alligators, also love aphids, and some species feast on scale insects, thrips, mealybugs, and mites. Aphids are also devoured by tiny braconid wasps and hover fly larvae. The pincer-jawed rove beetles eat aphids, too, and also feast on mites, fly eggs, and root maggots.

Insect allies of the gardener can be encouraged to live in a garden if there are enough diverse plants to attract their food sources (other insects) and allow them to eat at all stages of their life cycles. Predatory insects use a variety of means to capture their prey. Parisitoids such as braconid wasps get nourishment from another insect by laying their eggs on or near a host so their babies can feed on it as they develop. The tomato hornworm caterpillar, which consumes tomato leaves, fruits, flowers, and terminal shoots, is a familiar victim of this type of parasitism. Most parasitoids have very specific tastes when it comes to eating their culinary targets. This is helpful to the gardener, who can study which parasitoids it would be useful to introduce to solve specific problems as they arise in the garden.

Pollinators, such as bees, are especially important visitors to attract to a garden, and one mature flowering shrub can provide a bonanza for them. In return for the plants' nectar and pollen, these pollinators help our plants set fruit, providing food for other wildlife, who then play another vital role in the plants' reproduction by dispersing their seeds. Other creatures that help gardeners are classified as soil builders. They break down and consume leaves, twigs, and other organic matter, releasing this litter's nutrients into the soil. Of course the most famous soil builder is the amazing earthworm, which both aerates the soil and enriches it with worm castings.

Plants that are not indigenous to the United States are referred to as "non-native," "exotic," "alien," "ornamental," and "imported." Native plants are those that originated in this country and have survived here for thousands of years. They have evolved as they have adapted to particular regions of the U.S. and the geography, soil, and climate of those areas. As they evolved, so did the local insects and other wildlife that use them for food and shelter and as hosts for eggs, larvae, and nests.

When plants are imported from another country to ours, they are often advertised here as being "pest free" and extremely floriferous. This is because ornamentals that are very showy, in terms of flowering profusely, are attractive to gardeners like us who want to grow lots of flowers and different combinations of shrubs and perennials. These alien ornamentals can be attractive to native creatures in terms of nectar production, but they usually are not attractive to most of our native herbivores as food sources as they are not part of our long-established ecosystems. Our native caterpillars, for instance, limit their leaf consumption to certain host plants with which they have co-evolved. There are very few cases in which these host plants are ones introduced from outside North America. Additionally, plants and shrubs that have been introduced have very few natural enemies here to keep their growth in check. The result is that they usually flourish in our gardens, and look as beautiful at the end of the growing season as at the beginning of it. Few of our native insects have nibbled on their leaves, and the plants have thus not contributed to the reproduction cycles of our native insect populations. Who knows how long it will take for our native insects to develop a taste for the exotics? Meanwhile, if we gardeners are planting more and more ornamental shrubs and fewer natives, the few native shrubs we do have will look bedraggled by the end of the growing season. They have played a key role in the garden's faunal reproductive cycles without the benefit of a supporting cast of their own and other native species, and have had the onus of providing food for more and more insects.

If the exotic plant's natural enemies (e.g., insects and pathogens) have not accompanied it to its new home, a plant can become invasive, growing not only where it is planted, but escaping and thriving in other areas, including native ecosystems, where unchecked aliens out-compete native plants. They destroy the environmental balance of the ecosystem by creating a monoculture of themselves where there was once much biodiversity—of flora, and furthermore, its associated fauna. Invasive plants contribute to the danger of extinction for species already on the edge due to environmental degradation and habitat loss. Of course, the same phenomenon occurs in all areas of the world; plants native to North America may become invasive on other continents. Likewise, plants that occur naturally in one region of the U.S. may become a pest in other parts of the country. In each instance, the concern is not to maintain a "pure" native flora that is superior to others, but to preserve the biodiversity that exists in a healthy, self-sustaining environment that has evolved over millennia.

How, then, can the conscientious gardener grow exotic plants in a responsible way, and successfully incorporate them into a garden along with native shrubs and herbs?

- We gardeners can reduce the environmental impact of imported ornamental plants by making a conscious effort to avoid planting aliens that are identified as invasive species. See appendix N for a list. These plants pose a real threat as they can escape into the wild easily. Multiflora rose, autumn olive, and Asian honeysuckle are classic examples of invasive shrubs that have been spread far and wide by seeds excreted by birds who consume the fruits. Other plants such as Asian bittersweet and wintercreeper vine spread aggressively via runners.
- We can maintain a healthy balance between the number of benign alien ornamentals and the number of native species that we grow in our home gardens.
- We can design our home gardens so as to preserve more of our native flora and make it a priority to plant as many native shrubs as we can to provide food, shelter, and appropriate conditions for reproduction for birds, butterflies, and mammals.
- We can plant more flowering shrubs, as pollinators are attracted to all flowering plants. However, the more diverse our shrub plantings are, the better our garden will be as a habitat that nourishes birds and butterflies at all stages of their life cycles. For example, the spicebush (*Lindera benzoin*) not only is attractive to adult nectaring insects, but is the host plant for the spicebush swallowtail caterpillar, which consumes the leaves and draws them around itself as a protective tent. By contrast the nonnative (and often invasive) butterfly bush, promoted for attracting butterflies of many kinds, only provides nectar for mature insects—and nectar is available in many, many flowers, whereas food sources for larvae are more difficult to find. The native buttonbush, also a favorite of nectar-loving

insects, as well as a host plant for the hickory horned devil and the promethea moth caterpillar, is another viable alternative to butterfly bush.

- We can be aware of the exotic alien pests introduced to this country on imported ornamentals—for example, the azalea lace bug, which was introduced to the U.S. on evergreen azaleas from Asia, and the Japanese beetles that destroy many roses and other plants in our gardens. When alien pests come in on alien plants and there is not enough plant diversity in our yards to attract insects and birds to control them, the aliens reproduce rapidly. The hemlock woolly adelgid, accidentally introduced from East Asia in 1924, is a great threat to our native hemlocks, and has now moved into the Midwest on nursery stock. The widespread use of insecticides that kill beneficial as well as non-beneficial insects adds to the problem of allowing imported pests with few natural enemies to increase in great numbers.

- We can plant more native fruit- and nut-bearing woody plants that provide food for wildlife, such as arrowwood (*Viburnum dentatum*), black or red chokeberry (*Aronia* spp.), winterberry (*Ilex*), beautyberry (*Callicarpa*), elderberry (*Sambucus*), sumac (*Rhus aromatica*), and hazelnut (*Corylus*).

- We can add shrub plantings to our existing gardens to increase the biodiversity and to increase the attractions for wildlife.

- We can replace invasive plants in our gardens. For example, where we have used burning bush (*Euonymus alatus*) in the past we can plant the native wahoo, *Euonymus atropurpureus*, which also has pretty fall color, or the vivid red chokeberry or native blueberry. Remember, since we are thinking about euonymus, that the invasive creeper of that name, *Euonymus fortunei*, needs to be removed from our gardens. It is a rampant spreader, even climbing trees, and if it goes vertical, it produces fruit that the birds eat and disperse far and wide. It is a hard plant to eradicate. One method is to smother it with thick layers of newspaper, wetted down and then covered with mulch. The newspapers are left in place for a long period of time. When sprouts appear they can be sprayed with an herbicide. The eradication of this pest is not a task for the faint-hearted, but it is imperative to make the effort or one's whole yard can be covered with it in the blink of an eye.

- We can introduce spreading plants with a more genteel nature to replace the plants that are overly aggressive. For example, at the feet of shrubs we can plant patches of the native partridge berry (*Mitchella repens*). *Repens* means "spreading," and this little gem was named by Carl Linnaeus to honor distinguished American naturalist John Mitchell (1711–1768). It is a winsome little plant, about an inch tall, and produces small white flowers in summer. It grows in the shade in slightly acid soil, so it can enjoy sites under evergreens and other acid-loving shrubs. In the winter it produces drupes that can be white, pink, or bright red. Give it plenty of moisture when it is first planted, though it does like good drainage and often is found scrambling over outcrops of stone. It is surprisingly drought-tolerant once it is established, which is an added bonus. It can be used in holiday decorations, too, so it is a versatile plant to have as a resident in a home garden. Plant enough, using stem cuttings from the mother plant, so that the birds can share it. It has sweet little evergreen leaves touched with white at the midline.

- We can plant multiples of native shrubs that have admirable characteristics such as deer resistance and attractiveness to other types of wildlife. One in particular that is worth considering if there is space available is bottle brush (*Aesculus parviflora*), also known as buckeye. It is native to the lower Midwest and southeast into Florida. This coarse-textured deciduous shrub that tolerates wet feet will bloom in shade as well as sun and grows 8–12 feet tall in zones 4–8. It also grows to be wide in girth, suckers evenly, and attracts birds and butterflies to its spikes of white flowers in the summer. As if that weren't enough, it also puts on a show in the fall. If there is room for an avenue of these beauties, or if you want to partition off a secret garden of vegetables where the deer may not penetrate, this shrub is for you. Remember, though, that you need a large garden to accommodate multiples of these fellows.

- We can use boxwoods in much the same way as the large buckeyes—i.e., for edging smaller paths and areas if we don't have much garden space. Boxwoods are evergreen, do well in shade, and aren't attractive to deer. They are more restrained than the voluminous buckeyes, as they don't sucker or get blousy and are more formal in nature and habit. Still, they are perfect choices for evergreen hedges, avenues, garden room partitions, and so on. They also can be used as accents in a repetitive way. While Korean (smaller) and English boxwoods are not natives, they are well behaved and non-invasive and have the added advantage of having been model residents of North America for an extended time period while maintaining an unblemished record of restraint. In planting a shrub border or berm that will provide winter interest, combine boxwoods with conifers such as dwarf blue spruce in the foreground, with some holly (*Ilex* species) and some tall witch-hazel (*Hamamelis virginiana*), which has sweet fragrance from yellow flowers in fall.

- We can use the native deciduous shrub *Itea* 'Henry's Garnet' to form mass plantings and even serpentine hedges. These versatile deciduous shrubs are relatively small, have multi-seasonal interest, and grow in sun or shade. Their limbs when bare in winter make pleasing silhouettes.

HISTORICAL PERSPECTIVE

As we become more knowledgeable about ecology and sustainability and the essential role biodiversity plays in both, we see how native plants are an important element of the twenty-first-century garden. Not only do plants adapted to our local environmental conditions require fewer pesticides, less fertilizer, and in some cases less water, they also support native wildlife and help to counteract habitat destruction caused by agribusiness and urban sprawl. Our gardens are microcosms of the wider landscape, and what we each choose to plant or not plant in our own personal space has a cumulative affect on the health of our environment. Gardeners and their individual plots play an integral role in the effort to protect and conserve our local and also our global biodiversity. By planting a combination of noninvasive ornamentals and native shrubs, as well as edibles such as blueberries and raspberries (which can be incorporated into the ornamental garden), we can create landscapes that satisfy us aesthetically, delight us with the wildlife we attract, and provide locally grown food for us, while helping to sustain the ecosystem on which we all depend.

Jens Jensen (1860–1951), a Danish landscape architect who adopted the American Midwest as his home, was one of the first designers to advocate the use of native American plants in more naturalistic, sustainable landscaping. In his landscapes and gardens he emphasized fitting each plant to its environment, where it would grow with less maintenance (watering, soil amendments, chemicals), and fit into the local ecosystem.

It is relatively recently that uniquely American plants and designs have been valued in this country. Mid-eighteenth-century gardeners imported food plants and then trees, shrubs, and flowers from abroad to recreate ornamental gardens fashioned in the European tradition. This made the landscape look more familiar to the colonists, and more like the homes they'd left overseas.

English gardens and plants continued to be popular with American gardeners for a very long time. Many of the staples of cottage gardens even today, including lilacs, broadleaf evergreens, and roses, came from abroad. Meanwhile, some of our plants actually became popular overseas before they were seen as valuable or garden-worthy here. Our perennial asters are one example of this, as they used to be thought of as weeds here until the British starting featuring them in their gardens as Michaelmas daisies.

One of the very first native shrubs to be sold by nurserymen in the eastern part of North America was the westerner *Mahonia aquifolium*. Bernard Mc-Mahon began a nursery in Philadelphia in 1804 and was successful in growing the Oregon holly-grape, as it was called, found in the Northwest and grown from seeds brought back from Lewis and Clarke's expedition in 1804–1806. Actually it had been discovered by a man named Menzies some years earlier and by David Douglas, who marketed it. At first it was propagated with difficulty, and therefore it sold for the handsome price of 10 guineas. By 1914 good plants could be obtained for three a penny. Asiatic species were imported later (M. *japonica* and M. *bealei*). Mahonias are broadleaf evergreens that today are used in shrub borders and foundation plantings in zones 5–9. They like moist, well-drained soil in sun or light shade and grow 3 feet tall and as wide. In late spring/early summer, they produce yellow clusters of flowers that are followed by blue fruit that is attractive to birds. M. *bealei* should be avoided, however, as it has become invasive in some parts of the eastern U.S.

The early nurseries in Pennsylvania, Virginia, and New York imported many plants from abroad so that nowadays they are completely assimilated into American gardens, and do not seem like aliens at all. Americans were greatly enamored by the diversity of plants available from Japan after 1852. So many plants (many have the word *japonica* in their names) were imported into the gardening centers of North America from Japan that today there are probably more Japanese trees and shrubs in our gardens than specimens from any other country, even England. Plants from Japan and Korea are similar to some plants that grow in the southern Appalachian Mountains. Most Japanese plants are immune to disease in North America. For example, the imported kousa dogwood (*Cornus kousa*) is immune to the anthracnose disease that affects the American flowering dogwood (*Cornus florida*). However, on the downside, many Japanese plants have dominated the choices made by nursery staffs in North America to the detriment of some of our own natives. For example, the Japanese pachysandra (*P. terminalis*) is a ground cover that has been promoted heavily in this country. Our own native *Pachysandra procumbens* has not received equal billing.

We owe much to the valiant plant explorers of the eighteenth and nineteenth centuries who travelled far and wide discovering and documenting new trees, shrubs, and plants and bringing home specimens that nurserymen used to propagate new plants for the horticultural market. Gribbin and Gribbin (2008) have written about some of the most influential flower hunters who collected seeds and plants of species that we treasure today as mainstays in our gardens. Robert Fortune, for example, brought us azaleas, camellias, and, in particular, *Rhododendron fortunei,* which is named for him. This plant also played a significant part in the hybridization of rhododendrons in England. Fortune brought plants such as viburnums, magnolias, peonies, forsythias, weigelas, Japanese anemones, and Japanese mahonia back to England, as well as chrysanthemums and tea. He is also thought of as the creator of the black tea industry in India.

It was difficult for plant explorers to keep plants alive on long journeys. In 1834, however, an English physician named Nathaniel Ward found that sealed glass cases could carry plants successfully on long sea voyages. These cases were similar in principle to a terrarium and kept plants moist. Though trips are still made today by horticulturalists, the big one-person expeditions that made history are no longer in vogue. Rather, teams of representatives of institutions, such as national arboretums, go together on short missions—and of course travel is a lot easier, as well as communications between experts via the Internet.

Countries with large temperate regions where shrubs grow continue to supply the U.S. with interesting new shrub introductions. Our own North American breeders also continue to develop more "improved" varieties of well-known shrubs that promise characteristics such as pest and disease resistance and more profuse or colorful flowers (there is some debate about whether cultivars of our natives provide the same nourishment to wildlife as the shrubs' wild types). There are more shrubs and cultivars (cultivated varieties) available to home gardeners than ever before. This sometimes makes it difficult for the home gardener to maintain a balance of the exotics and the tried and true, the natives and the nonnatives. However, many gardeners are learning more about the virtues of some of our native plants and are trying to grow more natives in their gardens. As they do they are finding that many are more drought-resistant than imported ornamentals. So diversity is catching on as an overarching goal in modern garden design.

The Japanese beetle is undoubtedly one of our most reviled pests. It was brought into this country inadvertently and was first seen in New Jersey in 1916 on irises imported from Asia. It has no natural enemies here, since it is not a native; moreover, the females lay their eggs on lawns, and Americans certainly have lots of lawns. The larvae eat the roots of lawn grass and are fat, comma-shaped white grubs that all gardeners—it is safe to generalize on this—detest. When they become adults they eat the foliage of more than four hundred different plant species. To add insult to injury, they even mate while they are dining. Their appetites are so voracious that even sex does not trump food for these beetles. They have systematically progressed across the United States since 1916 and are still moving westward.

Other unwelcome visitors from Asia that behave like Japanese beetles and whose larvae also eat grass roots in lawns are the Oriental beetle and the Asiatic garden beetle. Though they look similar, they are not as colorful as the iridescent Japanese beetle. Unfortunately, they are equally destructive.

It is interesting, but not surprising, that these nonnative imported beetles destroy the imported prized exotics in our gardens that originally came to us from Asia. The foliage and flowers of the ornamentals that our native insects leave alone are absolutely ravaged by the Japanese beetles because they are part of the same ecological system. Roses and crape myrtles and hibiscus, to name a few of the shrubs they love, look very bedraggled once a swarm of these nonnative beetles have passed through a garden.

Other inadvertent Asian imports such as the sap-sucking emerald ash borer and hemlock woolly adelgid have had devastating effects on our native trees in recent years.

A SUCCESSION OF FRUITS

Shrubs are not only important in terms of the architectural permanence of a garden, as we have seen, but they provide many characteristics essential for the creation of a welcoming habitat for wildlife. Some native shrubs are often found growing at the edge of woods, in open areas such as fields, and beside roadways and bodies of water. Others are part of the understory in forests and form the middle layer between the canopy of large trees and the ground-hugging woodland plants, wildflowers, and groundcover. Shrubs often have a blanket of leaf mold and leaves around their feet that serves as a moisture-retentive mulch as well as habitat for some of the insects birds enjoy eating.

In wooded situations such as these, different types of birds will frequent each of the layers of vegetation.

Shrubs provide the most basic necessities for birds: shelter, nesting sites, and most notably food in the form of seeds and colorful, fleshy fruits. Although fruits are often uniformly called "berries," shrubs produce a variety of fruit types. A serviceberry is actually a pome, with a papery core containing seeds like an apple. A winterberry is a drupe, with a single pit like a cherry. A raspberry is an aggregate of small drupes. A juniper berry is a small, waxy cone. Blueberries and gooseberries, however, are actual berries, with fleshy interiors containing many small seeds. Shrubs provide an array of fruits throughout the year. For example, in autumn, our native deciduous holly bears red drupes on female bushes that persist into winter. Plant the wild type *I. verticillata*, or the male 'Jim Dandy' and the female 'Red sprite', as they are excellent cultivars of our native winterberry. The evergreen hollies also produce fruit for winter consumption. The roses provide rose hips that last into winter, too, and the sumacs bear long-lasting fruits as well.

See below for examples of fruits produced in other seasons.

BERRIES FOR BIRDS

Time	Common name	Botanical name
Early summer	Serviceberry/Shadbush	*Amelanchier*
Early summer	Chokeberry	*Aronia* spp.
Midsummer	Blackberries/Raspberries	*Rubus* spp.
Midsummer	Blueberries	*Vaccinium* spp.
Midsummer	Elderberries	*Sambucus* spp.
Midsummer	Gooseberries	*Ribes* spp.
Autumn	Dogwoods	*Cornus* spp.
Autumn	Viburnums	*Viburnum* spp.
Autumn	Mahonias	*Mahonia* spp.
Autumn	American beautyberry	*Callicarpa americana*
Autumn	Red chokeberry	*Aronia arbutifolia*
Autumn	Black chokeberry	*Aronia melanocarpa*
Autumn	Winterberry	*Ilex verticillata*
Winter	Evergreen hollies	*Ilex* spp.
Winter	Roses (hips)	*Rosa* spp.

- Fall fruits are important for migrating birds. Many migrating birds also eat insects, including butterflies and mosquitoes for protein. Bees and flies are attracted by flowers, and caterpillars, beetles, and bugs feed on leaves of shrubs.
- Try to plant more than one type of fruit-producing shrub. Plant 3–5 of each variety if you have space.
- Do not crowd these shrubs too closely together, as the fruits need sunlight in order to ripen. Prune back limbs of other nearby shrubs.
- Many shrubs offer nectar to hummingbirds (abelia, hibiscus, weigela, flowering quince, rose of Sharon, New Jersey tea, beauty bush, and American beautyberry).
- Goldfinches and tree sparrows enjoy the seeds produced by alders, which grow in wet soil. The seeds of buttonbush are relished by quail and waterfowl, and those of New Jersey tea are consumed by quail and pheasant.
- Sumacs (*Rhus* spp.) provide winter nourishment, as their drupes persist into the cold months.

Fruits of our native Euonymous shrubs (×2): Strawberry bush (*E. americanus*) and wahoo (*E. atropurpureus*). The lobed capsules split along seams to reveal a colorful fleshy coat, or aril, surrounding the seeds. *E. alatus*, the cultivated burning bush from Asia, is highly invasive and should not be planted.

Native Euonymous Fruits

Shifting tints of Hydrangeas

THREE

Bringing Flowers Indoors

She has taught us that you should be as careful in
choosing a vase for a flower as a dress for yourself,
and she has widened the term "vase" to include
almost anything that is, in itself, beautiful
and capable of holding water.

—*Beverly Nichols, foreword to Constance Spry,*
How to Do the Flowers

One of the enduring pleasures of having a garden is that we can step out of the door of our house and there it is. The garden gives us a special place to go, a break from the routine, a refuge from anxiety, solace in times of sorrow, and a soothing balm for our stress. It is our creation and yet it nurtures us even more than we nurture it. When we create a garden we create something so personal that it truly is like a part of us. We may even be able to understand why someone once said, "I can imagine leaving my spouse, but I could never abandon my garden."

FORCING BRANCHES

No one else knows our garden the way we do. We know where to look for the first crocus each spring. We remember the provenance of our plants, who gave them to us or where we bought them, and the day we planted them. When we can't sleep we let our mind drift around the garden and visualize what will bloom next, in our mind's eye. Oh, what lovely gardens we create in our dreams.

Perhaps one of the most precious gifts our gardens bestow on us is the joy of anticipation. It is especially intense each spring as we eagerly wait for the first tiny bulbs to appear, and the filmy green on the branches of our shrubs. We know which shrubs to watch. It may be a witch-hazel such as *Hamamelis* × *intermedia* (zones 5–9), a pussy willow, or a flowering quince or forsythia. We wait

for a warm day and signs of buds swelling, and finally that magical moment arrives and we cut branches and take them into the house to force them. It is easy and yet so rewarding. Cut some long branches, take them into the warm house, put the stems into a vase of warm water, and, hopefully, trick them into thinking it is time to bloom. If and when they do, it is our own private miracle.

Our garden gives us a private preview of spring, each year, to savor and enjoy. Forcing tall branches from our shrubs makes us even more eager to pick our first daffodils, and we can't wait to pick a fistful and bury our face in them. We rehearse the moment in our imagination, seeing them in a clear glass vase, or a blue one, or maybe in a rustic earthenware urn with tall branches from the early-spring-blooming *Spiraea thunbergii*. This spirea combines well with the bicolor daffodil 'Ice Follies', which also blooms early and has both white and cream colors to play off the tiny white spirea blossoms dotted along their bare stems. But any daffodils combine well with these dainty flowering branches. Any daffodils light up a house.

Arranging Became an Art

Documentation of elaborate flower arrangements in beautiful containers was first accomplished by Dutch painters in the seventeenth century. Not only were flowers and foliage used, but fruit and vegetables and insects also appear in these paintings and the results are sumptuous. By the eighteenth century, potteries were producing expensive vases for wealthy families. An elaborate vase of flowers was often placed on the mantelpiece. During the eighteenth century, explorers brought home to England a diverse array of exotic plants from all over the world. Conservatories and glasshouses were built to grow tropical plants year-round, and the Victorian gardeners and plant enthusiasts hybridized plants and produced a breathtaking array of gorgeous flowers. Ladies carried nosegays that complemented the colors of their gowns. The Victorians also used flowers to communicate, and a "language of flowers" was used to signal feelings and subtle meanings.

Flowers became a fixture on dining room tables, and silver rose bowls and epergnes were used as containers for massive arrangements in all of the public rooms of the grand houses. In the second half of the nineteenth century there were numerous publications that explained the art of flower arranging and contained pictures of arrangements for various events. Books and women's magazines provided tips on how to construct arrangements, swags, and garlands. Flower arranging became a popular hobby, as flowers were by this time available commercially for those without gardens.

By the turn of the century the Impressionist painters were painting beautiful flower pictures in which the containers were an integral part of the arrangements. They suggested the characteristics of the flowers and created a mood rather than realistic or botanically accurate representations of individual flowers. Some of the most well-known Impressionist flower paintings were those of the French painters Renoir, Manet, Monet, and Sisley. The colors of the vases were often colors that were similar to those of flowers. Post-Impressionists who produced lovely flower paintings were Seurat, Gauguin, Cezanne, and Van Gogh, who is so well remembered for those extraordinary sunflowers he painted.

Containers

The relationship between an arrangement and its container is crucial to the success of the outcome. The most basic lesson that has to be mastered is that of how the neck or opening of any container will support the flowers to be put in it. If we have a short-stemmed daisy and a long-necked wine bottle, the entire stem will disappear into the neck of the bottle and the flower head will just crown the opening. In this instance, of course, the scale of the arrangement is wrong. If we choose instead a long branch of forsythia in bloom, the scale will be much better as the cutting will provide a more satisfying proportion of flowering branch visible above the container's neck. In both cases, however, the narrow neck of the bottle keeps the flower upright. For one or just a few stems, narrow necks are best as they provide the most support to keep stems erect. If a few stems are placed into a wide-necked vessel, the flower heads will splay outwards and the arrangement will look awkward.

Supports

Props can be used to keep the stems of flowers anchored in a vase with a wide neck. In the late nineteenth century, inserts in the tops of vases were manufactured as an integral part of the container itself. The inserts had holes in them, and flower stems could be supported if each stem was put into or through a hole. Later, glass, ceramic, and metal inserts with holes for stems were manufactured separately for repeated use in various types of containers. They were called frogs, probably because they were intended to lie on the bottom of a vase submerged in water. Metal frogs with multiple spikes were also made, and when this type of frog is used the base of a flower stalk is impaled on one of the metal spikes. Scrunched-up chicken wire, glass marbles, stones, real or synthetic fruit, and even fresh vegetables can be used in tall glass containers. They anchor long stems and also show through the glass and add interest. Supports can match or contrast with the colors of the flowers and foliage in the arrangement. Some examples include a fall display of chrysanthemums with oranges supporting the stems and visible through a glass vase, or a Christmas display with red peppers in the vase's water and green evergreen boughs or holly held in place by cranberries, in a transparent container.

Oasis is a green foam available in blocks from hobby stores. It is soaked until the block remains on the bottom of a sink or bucket and no air bubbles are emitted. Then it may be cut to the size of the container. Each stem is then anchored in the foam. If a stem is too flimsy to penetrate the foam, a pencil is used to poke the hole into which a stem is then inserted. Oasis is only used once before being discarded, as bacteria will breed in it if it is re-used. If the plant material is tall and/or top-heavy and the container has low sides, an adhesive is placed beneath the foam in the bottom of the container. This strategy may be necessary to keep the foam anchored in the base of an open container before an arrangement is made. Florist tape (available in hobby shops), which is green and sticky on one side, can be placed on the top of a wide-necked vase to form a grid or checkerboard pattern into which stems are inserted. Or it can be used to bind the stems of a bunch of flowers together so that they sit appropriately in a vase. In both of the instances just described, one must be sure to have some foliage around the edge of the vase opening to camouflage the tape.

When Oasis was developed it revolutionized the way florists prepared arrangements, as it is inexpensive and easy to use. More recently, however, there has been some shift, among both individuals and professionals, away from using Oasis. More natural, reusable materials are gaining in popularity. For example, Rob Pattel, a well-known Dutch master florist, starts arranging by preparing a base of wet sand topped with moss, and into this he inserts branches, bark, stems, and kiwi vine to create his naturalistic designs that mimic "indoor fantasy gardens."

Straight twigs, such as those produced by willows, can be used also to fill about a third of a tall vase to anchor flower stems. These can be washed off and reused in the same manner that scrunched-up chicken wire can be reused. Ecologically conscious flower arrangers have coined the term *ecodesigners* and are currently advocating the use of more natural materials as plant supports. Many shrubs have twigs that are ideal for this purpose. Material harvested during winter from vines, such as climbing hydrangea and clematis, or twigs from the shrub itea can also be used in ecodesigns.

The Slow Flower movement is similar in some respects to the Slow Food movement. Increasingly, professional floral designers are making connections with flower farmers in their region and concentrating on buying more local, seasonal, and sustainable flowers. They are so much fresher than flowers that have been flown to this country from South America and Europe and they often smell better, as they have not been sprayed with chemicals.

Nothing, however, is fresher than the blossoms, foliage, and branches picked from one's own garden. A well-appointed shrub garden can provide a bonanza of plant material for the home flower arranger. It also provides opportunities to harvest many gifts for family and friends across the year. As the shrubs become established they can provide branches, at first, that are small, and these can be used for miniature arrangements. As the shrubs grow and have longer branches to be pruned, they will yield opportunities for more extravagant bouquets in tall vases full of boughs and branches.

BOUGHS AND BRANCHES

Most shrubs look well as cut flowers if tall vases are used and long pieces are cut from the shrub, as they stand tall or arch in the vase. Cut or hammer woody stems so the tough bark is broken and they can take up the water.

In Springtime

In springtime, use spring-blooming witch-hazel, the early-blooming spireas, flowering quince, flowering almond, the viburnums, mock orange, and mountain laurel. While most lend themselves to large and tall vases, some also look winsome when short pieces are cut for small vases. Small, flat vases with built-in pin holders are useful for displaying one interesting piece of azalea or rhododendron, as the arrangement can look like a small tree and have a Japanese affect. Mock orange looks refreshing when short/medium sprays are combined in a vase with one or three larger flowers in front near the rim of the vase. Always condition shrub branches in a bucket or sink of warm water for some hours before arranging them. Strip all leaves that will be submerged in water in the vase. Submerge evergreens such as holly and hydrangea foliage.

In Summer

Shrubs are useful when one needs a large flower arrangement to stand in the hall, or in the fireplace during hot weather. The scale is always important, as the top should not be so tall that the vase is in danger of falling over. The flowers should usually not be more than one and a half times the height of the container, or, said another way, the container should be one-third of the total height. However, one can judge best with one's eye.

Flowers can be bunched together in one's hand and then placed in an open-necked vase. Or the flowers can be arranged in a fan shape if the finished arrangement is to be against a wall. A flat arrangement on the back will look like an open fan from the front. Let some of the stems come forward to round out the front of the fan so that the display is three-dimensional. Use gray lamb's ears, opal basil, hosta leaves, and other green foliage to contrast with the pieces of flowering shrubbery. As you walk around your garden, snip pieces of various bushes and perennials and see how they look together in your hand. Experimentation is the best way to learn about new combinations and which flowers and foliage hold up best in a vase indoors. Change the water often and cut each stem to have a single flower rather than multiple blooms. This will ensure that individual flowers get sufficient water so that they don't wilt, and will extend the vase life of flowers such as lilacs.

To make a centerpiece, cut all of the stems the same length and insert them into a low bowl filled with Oasis to form a dome shape. For an asymmetrical arrangement to be viewed only from the front, be sure to choose a point in the Oasis where all of the stems are inserted together, so that it looks as if the flowers are growing from the same point. Use foliage to cover the rest of the block of Oasis.

IDEAS FOR EASY ARRANGEMENTS

1. Get a bottle and poke some long pieces of yew into it. If there is room place a candle in it and a sprig of holly with a short stem. Use Play-Doh on the inside rim of the neck of the bottle to keep material in place.
2. Find a goblet and cut some green Oasis (soaked in water) to fit the inside. Arrange pieces of spirea into the foam. Have the longest piece in the middle, and graduate the heights downwards on each side of it. Droop the last pieces on each side downwards. Place three flowers, such as roses, at a low (graduated stem lengths) position right in the center of the arrangement as the focal point.
3. Cut branches of hydrangeas and remove most leaves. Condition in water for about six hours after crushing stems so that they absorb more liquid. When ready to arrange, fill a pitcher with water and bunch the stems into the opening. Make sure the center flowers of the arrangement

are the highest and the sides are graduated in height so the bunch looks symmetrical.

4. Go to a hobby store and buy a bag of artificial oranges and lemons. Find a tall glass vase and place the fake fruit in it and fill with water. Put branches of forsythia, pussy willow, flowering quince, or even just branches of green leaves or fall-colored leaves in the container. The fruit will stabilize the stems in the same way that glass marbles do.

5. If you have a saucer magnolia tree, or other tree or shrub with interesting twigs, cut some to use for height in arrangements, especially in winter, when diverse textures are important for variety in arrangements of evergreens.

6. If you have a china shoe, china animal, or large seashell in which you could make a whimsical arrangement, fill it with sand and then pour water on it so that the wet sand will anchor your stems. Experiment with twigs and berries and odds and ends from the garden and maybe one or three blossoms placed low as the focal point. Always use odd numbers of stems.

7. For displaying arrangements try to find a base to elevate the vase slightly. Small black platforms can still sometimes be found in Asian stores, secondhand stores, or antique shops. Not only do they protect your furniture from watermarks; they enhance the arrangement. Other types of stands and decorative plates can also be used. Placing an arrangement on a pretty plate also allows easy cleanup of blossom petals that fall.

8. Put branches of delicate flowering beautyberry in a vase with purple coneflowers. The diminutive pink flower clusters of the beautyberry will soften the coarse coneflowers.

9. Buy a low, flat container that incorporates a small pinhead frog situated off-center. This type of container is invaluable for a quick arrangement of a single branch or bloom. You can also make a grouping of an odd number of stems, but always insert the stems so they appear to be coming from the same point in the frog.

10. Try combining blue-colored evergreen boughs with white hydrangeas, mock orange, spirea, and vitex or caryopteris. Sprays of weeping willows also combine well with upright branches of itea for a spiky contrast.

11. Try a tall all-green arrangement of shrub branches just as they are starting to leaf out. This can be combined with a couple of branches from the redbud tree also, or some dogwood or crabapple.

12. Combine branches of flowering broom with white pampas grass or ferns.

13. Use white vinegar to clean marks from inside glass vases.

14. Group small cranberry glass vases together and put dried flowers in them in the fall and sprigs of evergreen in December. Unify the arrangement by having all of the vases the same color or by repeating the plant material exactly so that the contents of the vases match. There needs to be one unifying element.

15. Check secondhand stores for miniature vases and small bottles to display small snippets of shrubs and tiny bulb flowers. Also look for vintage (1920s and 1930s) frogs. Glass frogs were made in the following colors: clear, amber, pale green, aqua, black, and amethyst. Some made in the 1940s and 1950s are referred to as post-war. Companies that made them were Imperial, Fenton, Viking, Hocking, Heisey, Fostoria, L. E. Smith, and Cambridge. All of these companies made Depression glass also.

16. Glass and pottery frogs have been made in Japan, England, Czechoslovakia, and Germany and exported. Metal frogs were made of lead, cast iron, pot metal (alloy), and brass and silver. Older types rusted, so water had to be changed daily. More modern types do not corrode. There are three styles available: pincushion (with spikes), hairpin (with tangled pliable wires), and flat mesh grids.

17. Collect cobalt blue bottles in which to display singleton stems or branches on windowsills or in groups on tables.

18. Witch-hazel twigs are pliable and can be collected to use in arrangements or as supports in vases.

19. In winter, gather greens from various conifers and broadleaf evergreens and wire pinecones to insert, together with holly, to make arrangements of various sizes.

20. A focal point is not necessary in an arrangement of branches and boughs in a tall vessel. However, in lower arrangements place one or three larger flowers, pinecones, or other eye-catchers near the center rim of the vase.

CHARACTERISTICS OF AMERICAN ARRANGEMENTS

At the risk of overgeneralizing, one could say that while flower arranging has components of religious and philosophic symbolism in the Japanese culture, Americans have not adopted that aspect of Japanese traditions. That is not to say that Japanese traditions have not been studied by American floral artists over the years. However, while the Japanese have very strict rules, American designers have always loved, and used, lots of color, unlike traditional Japanese flower arrangers, and have been eclectic with respect to using a variety of approaches and methods.

Again, generally speaking, Americans have been most influenced by the lines of Japanese arrangements and by the color and robust qualities of the European traditions.

Line

Design is the combination of many component parts in a manner that results in a visual gestalt that is pleasing and/or satisfying to both the creator and those who view the creation. The aim is harmony of line that meshes with both a container and a background. The elements in an arrangement include the plant (or other natural) materials, the container (with or without a stand), the background, and the accessories (small figures, drapes, trays, or other objects that may be an integral part of the whole display, but must not be distracting or dominating).

There are five characteristics in a completed arrangement: the shape (form, line, or silhouettes), the size (large or small and in appropriate scale), the mass (the quality of weight or airiness, darkness or light), color, and texture.

The simplest line in the Japanese tradition is three-dimensional. There is pleasing composition (unity), balance, and focus. The focus is the central point of interest in an arrangement, to which the eye is led because of the lines of the composition. It will usually, but not always, be found on the central perpendicular axis of an arrangement and often is near the rim of the container. Balance, i.e., the weight of the items placed on either side of the container's midpoint, may be either symmetrical or asymmetrical.

Naturalism

In modern American arrangements there is an emphasis on naturalism. Glass containers are favored so that the stems and supports are visible. As noted earlier, this is wonderful news for gardeners who grow a number of different shrubs in their yards, as boughs and branches of shrubs lend themselves to this naturalistic style. Arrangements are easy to make, and the aim is for the viewer's eye to seem to be looking through the branches of the flowering shrub itself.

The unifying components of some modern American arrangements are naturalism combined with repetition of single characteristics. These characteristics could include repetition of the color or transparency of containers that are grouped together and hold the same color or type of flowers—for example, a number of clear glass bottles of varying shapes and sizes, all containing one flower of the same type or color, in a tabletop or windowsill arrangement.

Sometimes the same blossoms will be massed (e.g., hydrangeas, pieris, zinnias), and sometimes individual flowers will be spaced so that their entire form (stem, neck, and head) becomes an individual piece of art. Line, as a principle in this type of arrangement, is approached by the repetition of many discrete lines, rather than the shape of the overall composition itself.

This current naturalistic approach to bringing nature indoors, as an organizing principle in the creation of arrangements, is liberating for gardeners. We don't need to study to become flower arrangers. We don't need to be intimidated by what others can do. There are no rules except that the display must look natural. We have probably always used our own garden flowers that are in season and they are certainly grown close to our homes. So we benefit from the current emphasis on seasonal blooms grown locally. And we don't have to worry, as our predecessors may have, about flower arranging rules! If it is homegrown and fresh, we can display it however we wish. We don't even need to take a course or apologize; we can just murmur that we are advocates of the naturalistic school of flower arranging.

The following is a sequence of materials the shrub garden can provide as the months unfold:

February

- Tiny sprigs of winter-blooming witch-hazel arranged in a miniature brown earthenware pitcher or eggcup. Can be grouped with miniatures of small bulbs arranged in other earthenware items, and size and shape can vary.
- A tall vase of pussy willow standing on the hearth or mantel. Or a smaller collection of pussy willow stems in a pewter pitcher.

March

- Small, flowering twigs of orange/pink quince poked into wet sand in a large seashell. Make sure the stems arise from the same point in the container so they do not look as if they are lined up like soldiers.
- Large boughs of forsythia in a tall vase on a sideboard or end table.
- Small branches of dark green yew in a low vase of daffodils, forsythia, or early-blooming spirea (this is the type with spires of arching branches dotted with small white blooms).

- Pieces of blue spruce combined with maroon hellebore blossoms.
- A collection of small white milk glass containers, each with one sprig of flowering quince, forsythia, or dainty early spirea.

April

- Pitchers of viburnum, daphne, redbud, dogwood, serviceberry, spicebush, itea, or ninebark.
- A massed vase of tulips with lilac boughs (strip off all lilac leaves).
- A tall vase of flowering almond or a low vase with late-blooming white daffodils, or mock orange or viburnum.
- Tiny miniatures grouped together, each containing a sprig of spicebush, mock orange blossom, or calycanthus.
- Tall boughs of mock orange arching from a narrow-necked vase or a blue or green glass bottle. Or use any other bush in bloom.
- A round centerpiece of magnolia blossoms

May

- A huge vase of spirea 'Bridal Wreath' (this is one of the varieties with round blossom umbels).
- A middle-sized bowl with stems of 'Miss Kim' lilac and short-stemmed peonies, inserted into Oasis closely, so no greenery is needed.
- One tree peony bloom in a medium-sized narrow-necked bottle or in a float bowl or wine glass.
- 'Queen of the Night' tulips with branches of the subshrubs gray sage or lavender.
- Dogwood (kousa), laurel, or sumac boughs in a rustic container.
- Dogwood sprigs in a medium-sized vase with purple iris.
- Double-file viburnums with blue baptisia flower spikes.
- Violas and pansies in small bottles and jars with daphne foliage or single vases containing only lacy leaves (such as Japanese maple) or variegated *Caryopteris* foliage.
- Dark foliage of ninebark shrub with green foliage from boxwood with a few purple pieces of catmint flowers.
- Pansy heads in a float bowl with foliage from daphne shrub.
- Three flowering plum branches in a tall, narrow vase.
- Masses of *Pieris japonica* in a midsize vase or pitcher.

June

- One full-blown, stemless rose in a champagne glass.
- Float any blooms in a shallow dish of water so you can look down into them.
- Cut hydrangea blooms and cut or split the woody stems at the ends to help them absorb water. Then arrange in a tall vase and mass together voluptuously.
- Cut short branches of *Daphne* 'Carol Mackie' and combine in a vase with large variegated hosta leaves.
- Put one large rhododendron flower in a float bowl. Cut stem off first.
- Cut branches of azaleas and mass in a wide-mouthed, medium-height container.
- Put a few tall alliums in a narrow-necked container or bottle.
- Cut pink spirea and put one piece each in as many glass containers as possible and make a tablescape on a large table.
- Make a delicate airy display of mint sprigs and meadowsweet in a pastel-colored container. Herbs add fragrance to bouquets.
- Take a small watering can and fill it with lilies and spikes of the subshrubs rosemary or sage.
- Create a vase of hemlock and monarda.
- Make a medium-sized vase of weigela with greenery as filler.

July

- Cut some single stems of black-eyed Susans and combine with opal basil, ligularia leaves, or evergreen foliage.
- Put butterfly weed and boxwood foliage in a medium vase.
- Cut a large vase of vitex for a hall table.
- Make a gray/silver arrangement using sage, rosemary, lavender, perovskia, and white oakleaf hydrangea blossoms.
- Cut some stems of blue spruce or other blue-gray evergreen and arrange in a glass vase with oranges or lemons in the water. Add a few yellow or orange flowers such as helianthus or butterfly weed if you wish.
- Combine Queen Anne's lace with gray lamb's ears, sage, rosemary, lavender, iris leaves, and baby's breath and/or gray-green evergreens.
- Make an arrangement of dry twigs stuck into a pin holder with one large zinnia as a focal point.

August

- Crape myrtle branches can be arranged in a narrow-necked vase.
- Cut a large vase of *Hydrangea paniculata* or any other hydrangea that is blooming. A little vinegar in the water helps them last at times when it is hot.
- Cut small branches of blue caryopteris and combine with any other flowers in your garden, as blue goes with most colors.
- Put one sprig of crape myrtle with one sprig of dark-leaved prunus in each of a series of small vases and arrange as a tablescape.
- Cut green-leaved branches of shrubs that have finished blooming and combine in a tall vase with opal basil and long stems of perennial asters.
- Cut spirea, if it repeat-blooms, to combine with other plants or stand alone on its own merits.
- Float individual impatiens flowers in a float bowl with small green leaves from any shrub you have.

September/October

- Combine asters with branches of any shrub that has interesting foliage in a tall glass vase with lemons in the water to provide support for the stems.
- Cut some sprays of callicarpa that have yellow foliage with purple berries. These will look good in any size of vase with gold- or brown-toned chrysanthemums, or on their own.
- Cut sage, lamb's ears, dill, basil, and mint for a pitcher of herbs for the kitchen counter. Add a few white chrysanthemums if you have them, or berries from fruiting shrubs.
- Use some pink or lavender mums and asters with lamb's ears or sage in a small or medium vase.
- Combine dark red mums, red fruits (e.g., holly or viburnums) and some large hosta leaves.
- Cut tall pieces of malva and combine with the foliage from astilbes, ferns, or mahonia.
- As shrubs lose their leaves, be on the lookout for interesting bare branches or twiggy bits to cut for winter displays.
- Cut globe amaranth and blue salvia and hydrangea to dry, hanging them upside-down. Also hang any hydrangeas you have blooming.

- Find an evergreen bough and expose the lower stem so it looks like a trunk. Place the branch in a square container with a frog so that it looks like an evergreen tree growing in a tub. For the holidays put winterberry sprigs around the trunk, or scrunch up red foil or put a red scarf or place mat under the container.
- Fill a low bowl with holly and insert a few red carnations, with stems cut short, into the greenery.
- Use singleton red flowers or spray roses in a grouping of glass bud vases on a table. Drape evergreens around the bases of the vases. A seasonal scarf could also be used to drape around the vases.
- Make a low arrangement of evergreens, bare twigs, and seedpods, and nestle one or three red roses as a focal point low in front.
- Make a solution of one part glycerin and two parts water reaching four inches up the stem of a bunch of leaves, e.g., beech, laurel, ivy, magnolia, rhododendron, or camellia. Split the stems first and place the branches in the solution in a place with good air circulation for three weeks. The foliage, preserved in this manner, will last indefinitely as a dried arrangement out of water. Individual leaves can be incorporated to hide frogs, or the leaves can be placed flat on plates when other fresh arrangements are made later in winter.
- Make a dried arrangement of yarrow heads, preserved leaves, and dry twigs.
- Place glycerin-preserved leaves, sparsely arranged, in a shiny black container or low vase on a hall table.
- Strip some of the needles from sprays of pine so that the stems are topped with brush-like evergreen pieces. Arrange with pinecones and small Christmas balls or ornaments.

SHRUBS YIELD OPPORTUNITIES

The more shrubs you plant in your garden, both native and nonnative, the more material you can harvest from your own yard across not only the three growing seasons but also in winter. Watch for times of the year when there is nothing blooming in your garden and try to find something that will bloom in that time frame. For example, if July is a low spot for your garden, make it a point to visit a nearby botanical garden or nursery in July to see what may be a possibility for your garden. If nothing that is blooming appeals to you, seek out a shrub with interesting foliage, color, or form to use as an accent. Also keep your eyes open and look at neighbors' gardens when you are going by, to see what grows well in your region. You will gradually fill in the blank times in your existing plantings. Look for dwarfs if space is tight or remove shrubs that are not paying their way.

GALLERY

How deeply seated in the human heart is the
liking for gardens and gardening.

—*Alexander Smith*

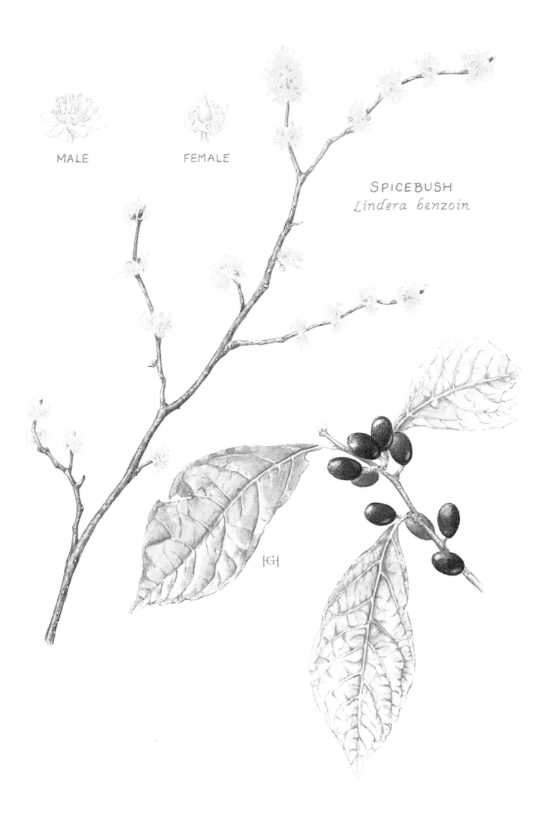

MALE   FEMALE

SPICEBUSH
Lindera benzoin

Spicebush

Lindera benzoin, commonly known as spicebush, is a native multi-stemmed understory shrub that grows as wide as it is tall. It has blue-tinted green leaves and a pleasing shape. New stems are upright while older stems stretch out horizontally. The fragrance of the leaves, bark, and fruit when crushed smells like spicy aftershave. The bright red fruit, which tastes like very strong allspice, was used for culinary purposes in colonial kitchens. Spicebush grows in swamps and moist woodlands from Maine to Michigan and south to Florida and Texas but is adaptable to drier sites and partial sun. It blooms in early spring on old wood and produces clusters of tiny chartreuse flowers that stud the bare stems. In full bloom the bush looks like a refined forsythia, with a softness that the brash exotic lacks. The spicebush has male and female flowers that occur on separate plants. The leaves appear after bloom and progress in size along each branch with the biggest leaves (obovate and 3 inches wide) drooping downwards at the ends of the branches. They turn golden in the fall, contrasting with the dark gray-brown bark. Female bushes produce shiny oval drupes that are showy in autumn, and are enjoyed by birds and other wildlife. Lindera is a host plant for the promethea moth and the spicebush swallowtail butterfly. The swallowtail's striking green caterpillar has huge yellow and black spots on its back that mimic snake eyes and help to drive off predators. Lindera is deer-resistant.

Zones	4–9
	Height 8–15'
	Width 6–15'
Conditions	Adaptable in terms of soil (acidic as well as somewhat alkaline) but prefers moist, fertile loam with part sun to light shade. Will grow in heavy shade with reduction in flowering
Landscape	Naturalizes well in swampy ground. Use at the edges of woods, in hedgerows and shade gardens, along streams, and in boggy areas
Pests and diseases	No significant pests. Deer-resistant

DOWNY SERVICEBERRY
Amelanchier arborea

Amelanchier (ah-mel-LANK-eer)

Serviceberry

Amelanchier arborea is a shrub or small tree with striated silver bark and delicate bunches of white flowers borne on bare twigs in early spring. The fruit is edible, sweeter and juicier in some species than in others. The common names are downy serviceberry, shadbush, or shadblow, the latter two references being to the migration of shad (fish) in eastern rivers that coincides with the spring blooms. "Service" is most likely a corruption of "sorbus." *A. arborea* and smooth serviceberry, *A. laevis,* are two species native to the eastern U.S. *A. humilis* is a native shrubby dwarf species. Amelanchiers are easy to grow in the garden, even in heavy clay soils, and they do well in sun and part shade. They are attractive throughout the year. Their leaves are gray-green and oval with a lighter underside that is downy in *A. arborea.* The flowers provide an early nectar source for insects and the small red pomes that ripen in late spring to summer are eagerly consumed by breeding birds, including cedar waxwings, bluebirds, and catbirds. Serviceberries have attractive pink to red color in the fall, and their bark stands out in the winter garden. They are hosts for caterpillars of the striped hairstreak, viceroy, and red-spotted purple butterflies, and are deer-resistant.

Zones	2–6
	Height 4–10' and as wide
Conditions	Adaptable to a wide range of soils and drought-tolerant once established
Pests and diseases	Leaf spot, rust, and stem cankers, but some cultivars are disease-resistant
Uses	Specimens
	Foundation plants
	The stoloniferous types are soil stabilizers

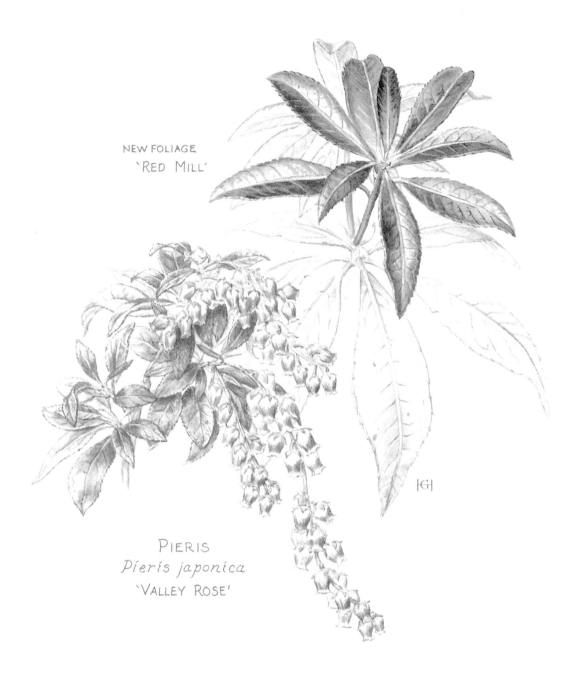

NEW FOLIAGE
'RED MILL'

PIERIS
Pieris japonica
'VALLEY ROSE'

Pieris (pie-AIR-riss)
Lily-of-the-Valley Bush

Pieris japonica is sometimes called lily-of-the-valley bush and is native to Asia.
It grows 6–8 feet in gardens but can grow to 12 feet and has flower clusters
that can be white or pink. Our native *Pieris floribunda*, commonly called
fetterbush, is found in mountain woods from Virginia and West Virginia south
to Georgia and grows up to 4 feet tall and 3 feet wide. It is hardy to zone 4, but
it does best in moist woodland soil with cool-to-moderate night temperatures
in summer. It does not suffer as much from lace bug damage as does the
Japanese import *Pieris japonica*. The lace bug was an inadvertent Asian import,
whereas *P. japonica* was intentionally brought in for its ornamental qualities.
P. japonica 'Avalanche' is covered by masses of arching sprays of little white
bells of sterile flowers each spring. It grows to 4–5 feet and as wide. *P. japonica*
'Valley Valentine' produces deep red buds and cascades of rosy-pink flowers
followed by new growth that is bronze in color. Other cultivars have red
new growth that is exceptionally showy. Pieris shrubs are evergreen and are
related to rhododendron and mountain laurel, so they can be combined with
these in woodland shrub plantings or partially shaded borders or foundation
plantings. A hybrid resultant from a cross of the Asian and American species
is *P. floribunda* × *japonica* 'Brouwer's Beauty', which grows to 2–3 feet. Pieris
is deer-resistant.

Zones	4–8
	Height 2–4'
Conditions	Part shade
	Moist, well-drained, acidic soil
Landscape	Mass plantings
	Woodland gardens
	Foundation plantings
Flowers	Flowers early spring, white or pink racemes. Deer-resistant
	Colorful new growth in some cultivars
Pests and Diseases	Lace bugs; fungus producing root rot

BLACK HAW
Viburnum prunifolium

Viburnum (Vi-BURN-um)
Black Haw

The black haw, *Viburnum prunifolium,* is native to the eastern U.S. and is just one of many viburnums easily cultivated in the garden. It has showy white flowers in the spring, and attractive leaves with pink petioles that resemble the foliage of cherry trees, hence the species name *prunifolium.* The fruit is a blue-black drupe, and the fall foliage is orange-red. It is a vigorous, fast-growing shrub that can become quite tall and rangy if not pruned. It is drought-tolerant and adapts to most soils as long as the site is well-drained. It grows in full sun as well as part shade, and is deer-resistant. A variety of other native viburnums grow well in the garden. Arrowwood, *V. dentatum,* is a more compact shrub that will grow in sun or full shade and prefers moist soil. Highbush cranberry, *V. trilobum,* with translucent red fruit, and nannyberry, *V. lentago,* both prefer moist-to-wet soil but will adapt to other soil types. The common name nannyberry refers to the blue-black fruit that resembles goat droppings. Possum-haw, *V. nudum,* is flood-tolerant, as its natural habitat is wet, mucky soil. Its cultivars are *V. nudum* 'Brandywine' (featuring a mix of pink and blue fruit) and 'Winterthur' (a more compact form). Ornamental Asian cultivars include *V. plicatum* 'Summer Snowflake.' It grows 6 to 8 feet and has a long bloom season, into fall. The compact, wonderfully fragrant Korean spice viburnum, *V. carlesii* 'Compacta', grows to 3 feet with pink buds opening to white clusters in spring. Use viburnums as specimen plants, in hedges, and as part of a mixed border. All viburnums attract birds, and their flowers draw in many pollinators. They are host plants for the larvae of spring azures and hummingbird clearwing moths.

Zones	2–7
	Height up to 15'
	Width 6–12'
Site	Well-drained soil, sun or light shade. Mulch to conserve moisture
Pests and Diseases	Avoid overfeeding. Clean up leaves to avoid mildew wintering over. Spray aphids with insecticidal soap. The viburnum leaf beetle is working its way south from Canada through New England, defoliating shrubs. Not all viburnums are deer-resistant
Landscape	Edge woodlands, screens, hedges, and specimens. Water during drought but avoid poorly drained soil. Best flowers and fruit occur in full sun to part shade

Dwarf Flowering Quince
Chaenomeles japonica

Chaenomeles (kih-NOM-uh-leez)

Flowering Quince

Chaenomeles japonica, with the common name of flowering quince, is native to Asia, has spiny branches, and can form a thicket 10 feet tall and 20 feet wide in full sun. The small, cup-shaped flowers begin to open in early spring before the leaves emerge. Flowers are arranged in orange/pink-colored clusters inside the shrub and the new foliage is often bronze in color. The old varieties produce large golden pomes that can be made into marmalade. Recently, many hybrids have become available that are more manageable and compact, especially those in the Double Take series, which have no thorns or fruit. C. Double Take series 'Orange Storm' and 'Pink Storm' have larger, camellia-type flowers in early spring on upright plants. They are relatively care-free and drought-tolerant in full sun, once established. They are also deer-resistant. The flowers can be forced indoors if picked as budded branches in late winter. The small varieties make good accents in borders and also do well as massed plantings, as edges for tall shrub borders, and as hedges. The species can be used for barrier plantings at the edge of large gardens, but the leaves may turn yellow if the soil is alkaline. The hybrids grow 3–4 feet and can be kept compact with pruning (prune only one-third each year) after they flower. Flowering quince is essentially a one-season shrub, so it does not need to be sited in a place that is prominent in the garden.

Zones	5–9
	10' tall and 20' wide, but dwarfs are available
Site	Sun to part sun in average well-drained soil
Pests	Scales and aphids
Foliage	Leaves may turn yellow in alkaline soil
Fruit	A few varieties have large aromatic fruit that is good for jam, especially C. 'Toyo-Nishiki' (grows 4–6')
Landscape	May be massed on banks and included in hedgerows

BLACK CHOKEBERRY
Aronia melanocarpa

RED CHOKEBERRY
A. arbutifolia

Aronia (uh-RON-ee-uh)
Chokeberry

Aronia arbutifolia, red chokeberry, and *Aronia melanocarpa*, black chokeberry, are both native to eastern North America, and offer four seasons of interest for the woodland garden. Both red and black chokeberries have clusters of white spring blooms with conspicuous pink anthers, attractive glossy green leaves all summer, strong fall color, and attractive branching during winter. They tolerate wet feet and poorly drained sites, but they adapt to dry conditions and sun or partial shade. They are drought-tolerant once established. Selective pruning to regularly remove old, thick stems is recommended. The red chokeberry is the most ornamental, with bright red edible fruits, brilliant fall foliage, downy twigs, and smooth gray bark. 'Brilliantissima' is a popular variety, and with judicious pruning it is an attractive garden shrub/small tree. The fruits of black chokeberry are very astringent and are often left on the shrub by birds until late winter. Because of their high level of antioxidants, however, they have become popular ingredients in juices, syrups, and teas. The chokeberries are larval host plants of the coral hairstreak butterfly.

Zones	4–8 (red)
	3–8 (black)
	Easy to transplant
Height and Spread	8' high and wide
Cultivation	Plant in spring. Divide spring or fall. Take cuttings in early summer. Sow seeds in fall (after removing fleshy coating). Needs good air circulation. Fruit production is best in full sun
Drawbacks	Tent caterpillars
	Produces suckers
	Some leaf diseases
	Plants become leggy, so prune after flowering to promote bushy shape

KOREAN LILAC
Syringa patula
'MISS KIM'

Syringa (sir-RING-guh)

Lilac

Syringa vulgaris, known commonly as lilac, is native to mountainous regions of the Balkans. It is a vigorous shrub and can achieve a height of 15 feet or more, and it bears trusses of sweetly perfumed blossoms. It has been naturalized widely through Western Europe. It probably came to North America before 1750 and was loved by the colonists for its fragrant flowers and because it survived both neglect and harsh winters. However, the common lilac often outgrows its space in small gardens. More recently developed dwarf varieties do not need the regular pruning that is demanded by the traditional lilacs. Bushes are usually multi-stemmed, and old wood and crowded interior stems should be period-ically thinned out. Dead flower clusters should be removed to prevent seed formation. Plant breeders have recently developed re-blooming lilacs such as S. 'Bloomerang', which is a dwarf that fits in small gardens and is suitable for a low hedge. The Korean lilac *Syringa patula* 'Miss Kim' is a medium-sized shrub blooming reliably in late spring and perfuming the garden. S. × *prestoniae* 'Miss Canada' blooms all summer, and 'Josee' is 4–6 feet tall and has lavender/ pink flowers that butterflies love. S. *meyeri* (4–8 feet) is one of the easiest to grow. It is drought- and pest-tolerant, and the small, glossy leaves have a pleasing texture. Lilacs bear trusses of enchanting pink, purple, white, violet, and occasionally bi-colored flowers. Unlike many imported shrubs, lilac does provide food for some native larvae, including the impressive hickory horned devil caterpillar of the royal walnut moth.

Zones	Hardy in zones 3–7
	Height can reach 10–15' except for compact varieties
Conditions	Likes rich garden loam but is adaptable. Needs sun and moisture to bloom well. Must have good drainage. Prune immediately after flowering
Landscape	Can be used in hedgerows and as accents. Smaller varieties are useful in foundation plantings, hedges, and borders. Plant where the scent will be noticed on patios, decks, etc.
Drawbacks	Borers and scale. The borer leaves sawdust and dead branches. Shriveled leaves indicate scale. Powdery mildew can also be a problem, so look for resistant cultivars

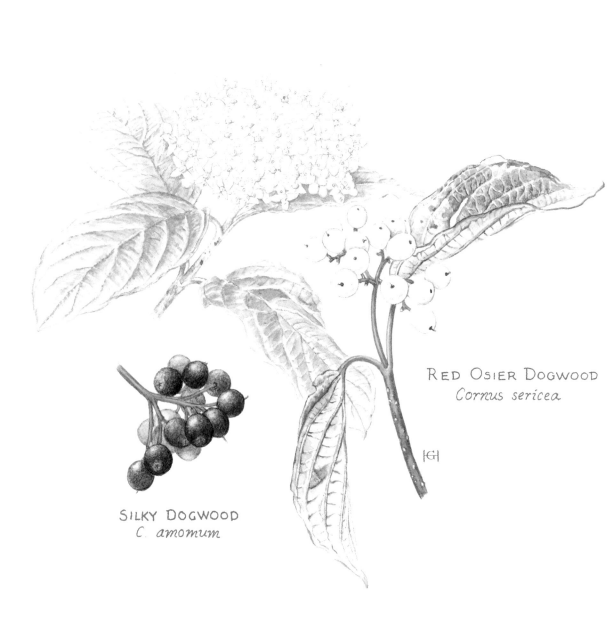

RED OSIER DOGWOOD
Cornus sericea

SILKY DOGWOOD
C. amomum

Dogwood

The genus *Cornus*, commonly known as dogwood, contains about forty-five species found in temperate regions of the northern hemisphere. They include herbaceous plants as well as trees and shrubs, deciduous as well as evergreen species, and have a lot of variation in adaptability. They are important food plants for insects and birds. One shrubby group native to the eastern U.S. has small panicles of white flowers and red stems that are especially decorative in winter. *Cornus sericea* (also *C. stolonifera*), commonly known as red osier dogwood, can spread into large clumps in swamps in the wild as it suckers. It has striking white berries with red stems. *C. amomum*, silky dogwood, is another native with similar characteristics but with cobalt blue fruit. Both of these shrubs have red autumn foliage, and their red branches make them great accent plants when combined with evergreens. In the garden, *C. sericea* benefits from being cut back to the ground in early spring. It does best in woodlands and hedgerows, as it is not a plant that fits in a formal setting. Two other native shrubs are roundleaf dogwood, *C. rugosa*, which prefers part to full shade and will grow on dry sites, and the shade-loving roughleaf dogwood, *C. drummondii*, which grows in a variety of soil types, including clay. There are also a number of native and nonnative cultivars, such as *C. sericea* 'Silver and Gold', with variegated leaves and yellow winter stems. *C. sericea* 'Farrow' Arctic Fire is a more compact cultivar with a height of 3–4 feet. 'Baileyi' is a non-spreader that is hardy to zone 2. *C. kousa* 'Wolf Eyes' is a Japanese dogwood with a height of 10–15 feet that forms a large shrub with showy flowers in June and that has gray-green leaves with a white edge. It has

Zones	2–10
	Shrubs and trees of varying sizes
Flowering	Spring-flowering (white)
Site	Sun or light shade. Variety of soils depending on species.
	Cut back multi-stemmed varieties annually for best winter color
Drawbacks	Dogwood borer and Anthracnose (affects only natives)
Landscape	Dogwoods are understory plants

large white flowers that resemble those of our native flowering dogwood (*C. floridus*) and pink-red fall foliage. It is slow-growing and can be pruned back after flowering in zones 5–8. The native dogwoods are host plants for the caterpillars of the spring azure butterfly and the polyphemus moth.

Buttonbush, spicebush, and lilac are included in the food plants of the Promethea silk moth caterpillar.

Promethea Moth

We cannot in fairness rail against those who
destroy the rain forest or threaten the spotted owl
when we have made our own yards uninhabitable.
Yet how quickly we could grow this land,
spangle it with blazing stars, stripe it with red
winterberries and white summersweet.

—*Sara Stein,* **Noah's Garden**

TREE PEONY
Paeonia suffruticosa

Paeonia (Pee-own-EE-uh)
Tree Peony

Paeonia suffruticosa is the tree peony, a shrub that has been cultivated in China since the seventh century. The more familiar herbaceous peony that dies to the ground each winter has been in cultivation since the fifth century BC. Peonies were imported by Japan probably by the eighth century and have long been propagated there so that Japanese varieties have emerged as quite different from those cultivated in China. The flowers have become a revered part of Japanese cultural ceremonies. They are found in temple gardens, and some are said to be three hundred years old. Tree peonies have always been more expensive than herbaceous peonies. In 1844 Robert Fortune procured nearly forty different varieties from China, and the British were then able to breed their own strains. Fortune (1812–1880) was from the Scottish border region and was the first plant collector to enter China after the signing of the treaty of Nanking. Tree peonies are plants that are grafted, so deep planting to encourage additional roots along the stem is recommended. They are tolerant of cold weather and will not grow in areas where winters are mild (e.g., California) or sub-zero (e.g., northern Minnesota or Canada). They enjoy well-drained soil and mulch to keep soil cool in winter and moist in summer. Unlike herbaceous peonies, tree peonies should not be cut back. This shrub makes a magnetic specimen plant for pollinators. Some of these shrubs produce flowers 6–10 inches wide with petals that seem iridescent, and some look like taffeta or silk. These plants are long-lived and should not be transplanted. They are handsome in a shrub border all year, as the striking foliage remains after the flowers have faded.

Zones	5–8
	Height 3–4' and as wide
Site	Full sun to partial shade with good drainage.
	Accents and foundation plants
Pests and Diseases	No serious pests or diseases. Deer-resistant
Flowers	Mid-to-late spring. Single and double flowers in pink, red, lavender, white, and yellow. Voluptuous in a vase either as a bouquet or as a single specimen

P. x virginalis
'MINNESOTA SNOWFLAKE'

MOCK ORANGE
Philadelphus inodorus

Philadelphus (fil-uh-DEL-fus)
Mock Orange

Philadelphus inodorus, a native of the eastern U.S. and commonly called scentless mock orange, is a classic garden shrub and has the largest flowers of the genus. It has oblong leaves about 3 inches long that are paired on arching branches. In addition to this native species, there are many other varieties and hybrids available. *P. × virginalis* 'Minnesota Snowflake' is a hardy hybrid with double flowers and a sweet fragrance. Mock orange is also native to southern Europe and Asia, and there are many hybrids that combine the North American and Eurasian species. Many were developed by the Lemoine nursery in France between 1884 and 1927. The distinctive feature is the perfume of the single or double white flowers in late spring that attract many bees and butterflies. Mock orange is tolerant of dry soil if well mulched and will grow in full sun to partial shade. After flowering, prune back to one-third and cut out old canes. It can grow to 3–10 feet tall, but not as wide, and can be part of a shrub border or hedgerow as it provides little interest when not in flower. Since this shrub has only one season of glory, plant a clematis that blooms at another time to weave through it. *Philadelphus inodorus* is a host plant for the caterpillar of the cecropia moth.

Zones	5–8
	Height 3–10'
	Width 4–6'
Site	Tolerant of many soil types. Prune to reduce size
Pests	No significant pest or disease
	Can be used as a cut flower in bouquets, corsages, and buttonholes for weddings

NINEBARK
Physocarpus opulifolius

'SUMMER WINE'

Physocarpus (fy-so-CAR-pus) NATIVE DECIDUOUS
Ninebark

Physocarpus is a small genus of about ten species, including *P. opulifolius,* or common ninebark, which is native to the eastern U.S. In spring or early summer physocarpus has clusters of small white or pink flowers. It also has decorative seed pods and fall foliage color. The common name *ninebark* refers to the shrub's peeling, multi-colored bark. It is a medium-sized shrub that can be pruned after flowering. Although it grows best on the banks of streams and loves moisture, it is adaptable and will tolerate almost any conditions, from wet to dry, acid to alkaline, sun to part shade. It has a strong root system, which makes it able to grow well in many sites, including wet soil conditions. The red seed pods mature in July or August. Some cultivars have dark purple foliage. A compact variety, *P. opulifolius* 'Little Devil', is 3–4 feet tall with a rounded habit and wine-colored leaves, and is excellent for small spaces. The flowers of *Physocarpus* bunch together and are easy for pollinators to land on. The leaves are eaten by the caterpillars of the spring azure butterfly, and songbirds like to nest among the boughs. This native provides excellent wildlife cover in the garden. It has multi-season appeal and can be used in shrub borders, as an accent, and in foundation plantings.

Zones	3–7
	Height 3–8'
	Width 4–6'
Flowering	Flowers early summer
Conditions	Tolerates wide range of conditions but prefers moisture. Adaptable and drought-resistant
Pests and Diseases	Untroubled by diseases and insects

AROMATIC SUMAC
Rhus aromatica

Rhus (roos)

Sumac

Our native sumacs are often overlooked when shrubs are being considered for home gardens, but plants in the *Rhus* genus show such vibrant foliage colors in autumn, and their handsome compound leaves in summer and deep red fruit in winter make them worthy candidates for naturalistic plantings. Aromatic sumac, *Rhus aromatica*, is a low-growing species ('Gro-Low' is a dwarf cultivar) that can be grown on sunny, dry slopes, as it is drought-tolerant. Winged or shining sumac, *R. copallina*, staghorn sumac, *R. typhina*, and smooth sumac, *R. glabra*, can grow to the size of small trees. They prefer well-drained soil and full sun, although they also grow on woodland edges. Sumac flowers are on greenish, yellow, or pink panicles that attract insects. Most sumacs require separate male and female shrubs for fruit production, but occasionally the aromatic sumac has both male and female flowers on one plant. In fall there are clusters of red drupes covered in hairs on most species. Poison sumac is in the same family but is usually placed in a different genus, *Toxicodendron*. It has smooth white fruits and grows in swamps and fens, so is not often encountered. All sumacs, whether "poison" to people or not, are great shrubs for wildlife, who relish the fruit. They are magnets for birds, who search the foliage and flowers for insects in spring and summer, and the persistent fruit helps to carry wildlife through the winter. The leaves provide food for larvae of the showy emerald moth and royal walnut moth (the hickory horned devil caterpillar).

Zones	2–10
Conditions	Adaptable in terms of soil and site. Likes full sun to light shade. Drought-tolerant/multi-season interest. Fruit (only on female plants) is attractive to wildlife. Choose those with red fruit. Height and spread depend on species. One good hybrid is Rhus × pulvinata 'Red Autumn Lace'. Cutleaf forms of smooth sumac exist
Drawbacks	Strong spreading habit in some varieties

VIRGINIA SWEETSPIRE
Itea virginica
'HENRY'S GARNET'

Virginia Sweetspire

Itea virginica is a summer-blooming shrub native to the lower Midwest and the southeastern United States. It is commonly called Virginia sweetspire. It has alternate leaves that are oval and narrow and glossy and that turn mahogany red in the fall. It grows to 5–10 feet, but *I.* 'Little Henry' is a compact 2–3-foot cultivar with masses of spiral white flower-heads beginning in early summer. Found in swamps and stream banks and moist woodland settings from southern New Jersey to Florida and north along the Mississippi valley into southern Illinois, it is adaptable and hardy to zone 5. It is tallest and most vigorous in the southernmost part of its range. It is a suckering shrub that can be renewed by cutting it back to the ground from time to time. The most popular cultivar in home gardens is 'Henry's Garnet', which has fragrant white racemes of flowers in June and garnet fall foliage. The flowers are fragrant and attractive to butterflies. The name 'Henry' in many of the popular cultivars refers to Mary Henry, who found 'Henry's Garnet' in the Georgia woodlands in 1954.

Zones	5–9
Site	Foundation plantings
	Specimens and shrub or perennial borders
	Good companion of Clethra
Conditions	Likes consistent moisture and will grow in soggy soil. Sun to light shade. Highly adaptable to heat and drought

SWEET SHRUB
Calycanthus floridus

Calycanthus (Kalee-CAN-thus) NATIVE DECIDUOUS
Carolina Allspice or Sweet Shrub

Calycanthus floridus, with the common names of Carolina allspice, sweet shrub, and strawberry bush, was first described in 1726 by Mark Catesby. He said it grew in the hilly and uninhabitable areas of Carolina. It is also native to the lower Midwest and the eastern U.S. from New York to Florida. By the 1750s it was being cultivated around Charleston and was also being exported to England. It produces stiff-looking maroon-colored flowers May through July that are unique but not particularly showy, and that have an unusual strawberry aroma that attracts pollinating beetles. The leaves, wood, and bark smell like cinnamon and remain fragrant when dried. Because the sepals and petals have the same shape and color, the name *Calycanthus*, meaning "calyx-flower," was given to the genus. Sweet shrub grows 4 to 7 feet, doing best in moist soil. It prefers full sun, but will grow in partial shade. It may be pruned after flowering, but it forms interesting seed pods if left unpruned. It is very resistant to disease and insect pests. Little attention has been paid to *Calycanthus* by plant hybridizers. There is another species, *C. occidentalis* (California sweet shrub), which does not flower as well as *C. floridus.* Most flowers appear in late spring, with occasional flowers during summer. There is a cultivar, 'Athens', which has yellow flowers. The Cherokee used Calycanthus as a medicinal and perfume. Sniff before you buy, as plants vary in fragrance.

Height and spread	4–10' tall and nearly as wide. Is shorter in full sun
Zones	4–9
Landscape use	Plant near seating areas in garden to enjoy fragrance. Plant in shrub borders and woodland edges
Site	Well drained, moisture-retentive humus-rich soil. Full sun to light shade
Foliage interest	Glossy green leaves that turn bronze or purple in fall
Pests and diseases	Rarely threatened by pests

SWEET PEPPER BUSH
Clethra alnifolia

Clethra (KLETH-ruh)

Summer Sweet or Pepper Bush

Clethra alnifolia, commonly called summer sweet or pepper bush because the black seeds resemble peppercorns, is native to the southeastern and Atlantic coastal areas of the U.S. In the wild it grows in swamps and moist woods. These shrubs can grow between 3 and 8 feet tall and almost as wide, depending on the species or cultivar. White or pink fragrant flowers borne in narrow, upright clusters appear in mid-to-late summer. They bloom well in sun or shade, and plants are late to break dormancy after winter. Clethra should be planted in the spring in well-drained soil and pruned in late winter. It is sometimes slow to become established and seems to do best in moist, acid soil, so it should be well mulched to conserve moisture and planted in partial shade where summers are hot. *C. alnifolia* 'Ruby Spice' has deep pink blooms. The foliage turns yellow in autumn. *C. alnifolia* is native to mountainous regions and forms a large, multi-stemmed shrub in the high elevations. Though hardy to zone 5 it dislikes heat and drought, so it needs shade in the heat of day. It has cinnamon-colored bark and fragrant flower clusters that attract bees, butterflies, and hummingbirds.

Zones	4–9
	Height 3–8'
Blooms	Mid-to-late summer, whites and pinks
	Fragrant
Plant in spring	Blooms in summer
Site	Well-drained soil
	Sun to part shade
Pests and Diseases	No serious pests or diseases
Landscape	Hedges, shrub borders, woodlands

CHASTE TREE
Vitex agnus-castus

Chaste Tree

Vitex agnus-castus has five leaves and is commonly called chaste tree. *Agnus* is Latin for lamb and *cast* is Latin for pure; hence the common name. Medicinally this plant has been used to treat ailments of the female reproductive system. According to folklore, medieval monks also used vitex seeds to quell their sexual urges. In most varieties the leaves are compound, with five leaflets radiating from the stalk, but occasionally the leaves are simple. Vitex forms a rounded shrub or small tree with upright branching. It produces erect sprays of 12-inch-long lavender-violet-blue flowers in summer into early fall. White or pink-flowered and variegated-leaf forms are also seen. V. 'Latifolia' has broader leaves. The flowers have an astringent, slightly medicinal perfume, and although the flowers look attractive in bouquets, the scent is sometimes too strong to allow them to be brought indoors. The aroma, however, makes them deer-resistant, and the charming color of the blooms in summer makes the shrub a good focal point in the landscape. It is excellent planted in berms and borders with other tall summer perennial bloomers such as helianthus. Gray-leaved plants also make harmonious companions. Vitex blooms at a time when few other shrubs are in flower. Plants grow larger in warmer areas but are killed to the ground in cold regions. May be cut to the ground in late fall each year in northern zones. The white V. 'Alba' is an excellent accent plant. This shrub is underutilized in gardens and adds a glossy and lacy texture to the plantings.

Zones	6–10 (with protection)
	Height 8–10'
Conditions	Adapts to most soils but does best in fertile, well-drained soil with plentiful moisture in the summer. A protected location with full sun is optimal. Propagate from seed in fall or spring and cuttings in the summer
Pests and Diseases	No significant pests and diseases
Foliage	Attractive green glossy foliage

×4

BEAUTYBERRY
Callicarpa americana

Callicarpa (cal-ee-KAR-puh)
American Beautyberry

Callicarpa americana, native to the southeastern U.S., is commonly known as American beautyberry, and is valued for its shiny, dark lavender-colored fall fruits. The tiny drupes grow in clusters along the bush's arching stems and last two to three weeks after the leaves fall. The diminutive white or pink flowers form in the leaf axils in midsummer and progressively open toward the branch tip. This shrub is really eye-catching in the late summer and fall, when the foliage turns yellow and the pinkish-purple fruits are most lustrous, creating a spectacular display. It has a mounding, open habit and the fruits form repeated clusters along the upper surface of the branches. Grow these shrubs en masse for better pollination. Fruiting is also heaviest if there are a few hours of direct sun. Vigor is maintained if these shrubs are cut back to the ground in late winter after the birds have finished with the fruit. In cold climates the shrub freezes to the ground and starts up afresh the following spring. These shrubs have an arching habit. It is best to plant callicarpa in its own dedicated area, as it spreads. *Callicarpa japonica* is native to Japan and tolerates light shade, though it prefers full sun. A Korean species, C. *dichotoma* 'Early Amethyst', sets its fruit earlier than other callicarpas (zones 5–8).

Zones	6–10
	Height 3–8'
	Width 3–6'
Site and Conditions	Likes well-drained soil but will tolerate drought. Needs some sun to fruit. Will grow in zone 5 with protection. Propagate by cuttings or ground-layering. Usually plants increase and may need periodic thinning. Mulch well or site near foundation at the limit of their hardiness range
Pests and Diseases	Scale insects
Landscape	Use in shrub borders and as screens. Attractive as foundation plants near stone walls and buildings. Mainly of interest in fall and not noticeable in other seasons

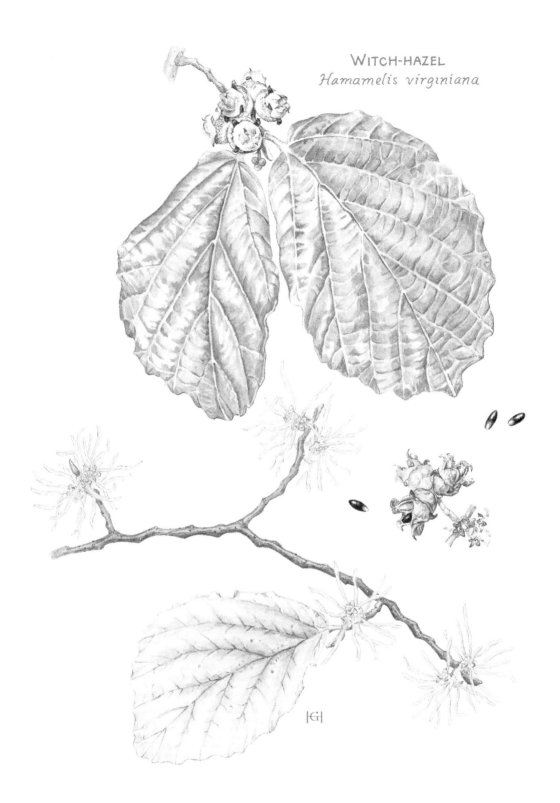

WITCH-HAZEL
Hamamelis virginiana

Autumn-Blooming Witch-Hazel

Hamamelis virginiana, commonly known as witch-hazel (sometimes called autumn-blooming witch-hazel to distinguish it from other species), is native to woodlands and edges of the eastern U.S. It bears spidery golden flowers when its leaves have turned yellow and are beginning to fall. Witch-hazels are multi-stemmed understory shrubs, and their leaves are oval and textured with visible veining in a fishbone pattern. The leaves are bronze when they emerge and then turn green. The buds are borne in the leaf axils, and if they are pollinated, capsules develop in the flower calyx. The bark has traditionally been steeped in water to make an astringent. The common name *witch* is derived from the root word for wicker, and refers to the pliable nature of the branches. This flexibility makes them useful in dowsing for underground water sources, known as "water-witching." *Hazel* refers to the shrub's similarity in appearance to the hazelnut, *Corylus*. *H. vernalis*, or the native spring-blooming witch hazel, ranges from Missouri to Texas, and bears yellow/bronze to deep red flowers with four wispy petals in late winter. These are prized by winter-weary flower arrangers for forcing. It suckers more than *H. virginiana* but does not grow as tall. In the wild both autumn- and spring-blooming witch-hazels are found in damp woods and thickets, and the two species grow together on the Ozark Plateau. Their seed capsules, when split open, reveal four shiny black seeds surrounded by a membrane. When the membrane dries out it contracts, causing the seeds to shoot out a great distance. The autumn bloomer has larger flowers than the spring bloomer and both have a light, pleasant fragrance. The most popular hybrid is *Hamamelis* × *intermedia*, and 'Arnold Promise' is a variety with large bright yellow flowers with red centers. It can be used as a specimen plant. Witch-hazel is a host plant for the caterpillars of the striped hairstreak butterfly.

Zones	4–5
	Height 8 to 20' and as wide
Site	Moist-to-wet or moderately dry soil as they are native to floodplains, damp woods, and thickets. Blooms best in sun
Landscape	An easy and adaptable plant for home gardens. May need rejuvenation pruning after 5 years, and needs space as it spreads branches horizontally. Use for woodland edges or hedgerows
Pests	No significant pests

MALE

×3

FEMALE

WINTERBERRY
Ilex verticillata

IGH

Winterberry

Ilex verticillata, commonly known as winterberry, is our native deciduous holly and grows in moist woods and swamps from Newfoundland to Florida, and west to Minnesota. In the Midwest it is commonly known as Michigan holly. It can grow 6–15 feet in the wild and up to 10 feet wide. Smaller cultivars have been developed, however, and the new cultivars usually suit home gardens best. As with the evergreen hollies, one needs a male to allow the females to bear the lustrous red spires of drupes that are so dramatic in the fall and winter landscape. It is hardy through zones 3–9 in sun to light shade but needs moist soil, especially to establish well, so do not plant on a bank or where the ground dries out. It has greenish white small blooms in the spring. The leaves are green and oval and slightly puckered. When first planted this shrub looks stiff and upright, but with age it becomes more open and rounded. It has smooth silver bark. The leaves have a burgundy fall color but drop early to expose the fruit, which is the major attraction of this shrub. In recent years many new cultivars have been developed, as the fruits are such a stunning fall feature in the garden, almost until Christmas. The birds will have finished them off by snowfall unless you plant a large number of these shrubs. If a neighbor has a male within a short distance you may not need to plant one, as bees can pollinate from a male about 60 feet away. A ratio of one male for twelve females will work well. Branches of these fruits can be used in indoor holiday arrangements. 'Jim Dandy' is a male that can be planted with the female glossy-leaved 'Red Sprite', and a pair of cultivars are 'Southern Gentleman' and 'Winter Red'. Hybrids resulting from a cross between *I. verticillata* and the Japanese *I. serrata* have also been developed. Deciduous holly is a must-have shrub for winter interest in a garden.

Zones	3–9
Size	Can grow up to 15' but smaller varieties are now available
Conditions	Prefers moist acid soil but adaptable as long as watered well when first getting established. Grow in full sun to part shade and plant a male with female plants to ensure pollination for fruit production. Varieties with orange fruit (I. 'Winter Gold') are also available but the red fruit is spectacular and highly prized for holiday decorations indoors
Landscape uses	Plant with shorter shrubs in front of a massed shrub border or in a berm. Or use as accents in perennial borders
Pests	No significant pests

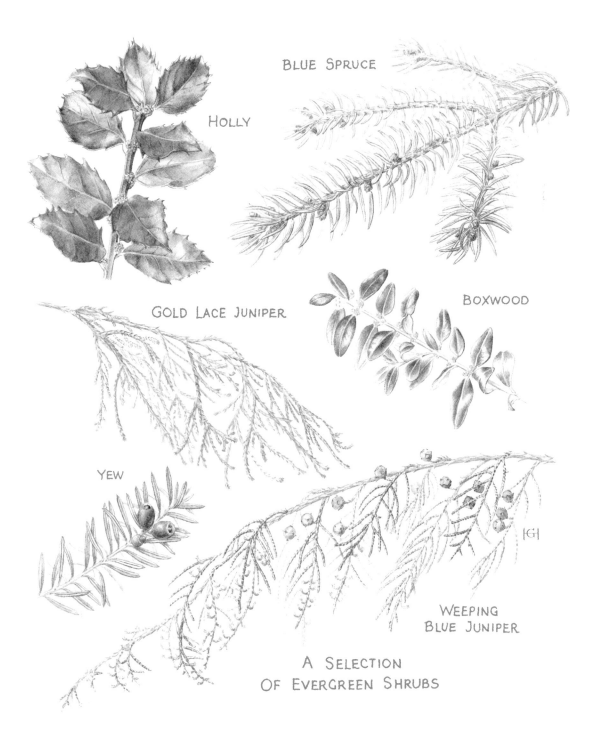

HOLLY

BLUE SPRUCE

GOLD LACE JUNIPER

BOXWOOD

YEW

WEEPING
BLUE JUNIPER

A SELECTION
OF EVERGREEN SHRUBS

Evergreen shrubs provide continuity of structure in the garden across the entire year. However, they are especially valuable in winter, when their mass, depth of color, varied textures, and silhouettes contrast with the bare-limbed woody outlines of the deciduous trees and shrubs. There are so many sizes, colors, and shapes available that it is hard to choose which ones to use as group plantings and accents. The broadleaf evergreen shrubs (e.g., rhododendron) contribute both shiny and matte surfaces, the boxwoods have small, neat leaves, and the conifers present us with both lacy and dense needle patterns. Always choose an evergreen that suits the site and conditions and always check the height a shrub will attain at maturity. *Thuja orientalis*, commonly known as dwarf golden arborvitae, is globe-shaped with golden-yellow branches all year. Hardy to zone 6, it is tolerant of heat, cold, and dry conditions but doesn't enjoy visits from dogs. This is important to know before planting. *Pica glauca* 'Conica' is a dwarf Alberta spruce and grows only 6 inches a year. The needles are bright green when new but then turn gray-green. The principle of repetition is important when planting a number of evergreens on a property. In order to integrate the shrubs into an harmonious whole it is helpful to repeat characteristics such as shape and color. Resist the impulse to plant one of every shape and size, as the overall effect may appear to be erratic. Try to visualize the shapes of the evergreens when they are covered with snow, and think about whether the plantings are the right scale for the home and landscape, both now and when they are fully grown.

If a person cannot love a plant
after he has pruned it,
then he has either done a poor job
or is devoid of emotion.

—*Liberty Hyde Bailey*

Appendixes

Appendix A. Pruning

Shrubs that bear their flowers on new growth (commonly referred to as new wood) in spring or summer can be cut down in late fall, winter, or very early spring. Since the new buds do not occur on the old branches, pruning before any new growth has begun will not affect the new season's bloom. Note that hydrangeas used to all bloom on old wood that wintered over from the previous year. Nowadays, there are new varieties that bloom on new wood as well as old wood. For that reason, gardeners need to ascertain the bloom pattern of hydrangeas by researching carefully before taking up the pruning shears.

BLOOM ON NEW GROWTH

Abelia	*Hypericum*	*Rosa* spp.
Barberry (*Berberis*)	*Indigofera*	Willow (*Salix*)
Butterfly bush (*Buddleia*)	*Kerria*	Meadowsweet (*Spiraea*)
Beautyberry (*Callicarpa*)	Crape myrtle (*Lagerstroemia*)	Chasteberry (*Vitex*)
Bluebeard (*Caryopteris*)	*Lespedeza*	*Weigela* (prune lightly)
Sweet pepper bush (*Clethra*)	Privet (*Ligustrum*)	Franklinia
Hibiscus	Honeysuckle (*Lonicera*)	Sumac (*Rhus*)

BLOOM ON LAST YEAR'S GROWTH

Azalea	*Deutzia*	*Rosa* (climbers)
Cercis	*Forsythia*	Lilac (*Syringa*)
Chaenomeles	*Magnolia*	(*Paeonia*)
Daphne	*Philadelphus*	*Viburnum*

SUBSHRUBS

Lavender (*Lavendula*)
Culinary Sage (*Salvia*)
Russian sage (*Perovskia*)

Appendix B. Shrubs by Season of Interest

NOTE

Of course a shrub that has more than one season of interest is always the best choice. Forsythia, while gorgeous in the spring when it flowers early and exuberantly, is quite unremarkable for the rest of the year. Site it in a spot where it is not center stage.

Spring flowers	Zones	Conditions
Tree peony (*Paeonia*)	4–8	Full sun/part shade
Viburnum spp.	5–8	Sun
Daphne 'Carol Mackie'	4–8	Sun/part shade
Serviceberry (*Amelanchier*)	5–8	Sun
Mountain laurel (*Kalmia*)	4–8	Sun/part shade
Kalmea latifolia 'Sarah'	5–9	Part shade

Autumn color	Zones	Conditions
Sweet pepper bush (*Clethra*)	3–9	Full sun
Serviceberry (*Amelanchier*)	4–8	Full sun
Chokeberry (*Aronia*)	5–8	Sun/partial shade

Winter	Zones	Conditions
Corylus contorta (Harry Lauder's walking stick—contorted branches)	3–8	Sun or shade
Willow (*Salix*—golden stems)	2–8	Sun/part shade
Dogwood (*Cornus stolonifera* or *amomum*) (red stems)	5–9	Sun/part shade
Cornus alba 'Sibirica' (red stems)	5–9	Sun/part shade
Pyracantha (fruit)	4–8	Sun
Holly (*Ilex crenata* 'Sky Pencil') (shape)	4–8	Sun/part shade
Ilex verticillata (red fruit)	4–7	Sun

Appendix C. Shrubs for Small Gardens

COLUMNAR GROWTH

Japanese Cherry (*Prunus* 'Amanogawa')
Juniper (*Juniperus scopulorum* 'Skyrocket')
Juniper (*Juniperus communis* 'Hibernica')
Yew (*Taxus baccata* 'Fastigiata Aurea')
Monterey Cypress (*Cupressus macrocarpa* 'Goldcrest')

DWARF CONIFERS

Arborvitae (*Thuja orientalis* 'Aurea Nana')
Arborvitae (*Thuja occidentalis* 'Rheingold')
Sawara Cypress (*Chamaecyparis pisifera* 'Filifera Aurea')
Juniper (*Juniperus squamata* 'Blue Star')

DECIDUOUS SHRUBS

New Jersey Tea (*Ceanothus americanus*)
Cotoneaster horizontalis
Aromatic Sumac (*Rhus aromatica*)
Hydrangea serrata 'Bluebird' (poisonous)
Abelia spp. (keep pruned)
Common Heather (*Calluna vulgaris* 'County Wicklow')
Broom (*Cytisus* × *praecox* 'Albus'—poisonous)
Hibiscus syriacus 'Blue Bird' or 'Hamabo' (pink)
Shrubby Cinquefoil (*Potentilla fruticosa* 'Pretty Polly')
Spiraea japonica 'Goldflame' or 'Shirobana'
Weeping Bald Cypress (*Taxodium distichum* 'Cascade Falls', a deciduous conifer)

EVERGREENS

Erica spp. (low-growing)
Candytuft (*Iberis sempervirens*—subshrub)
Shrubby Dusty Miller (*Senecio vira-vira*—subshrub)
Juniper (*Juniperus* 'Gold Cone'—narrow)
Dwarf arborvitae (*Thuja occidentalis* 'Fire Chief'—4' tall and wide)
'Howell's Dwarf Tigertail' (*Picea alcoquiana*—a 6' spruce)

Appendix D. Shrubs with Colorful Foliage for Accents

Golden foliage is useful on a shrub year-round, so do not just rely on shrubs with autumn foliage change. There are now many cultivars with golden foliage to choose from. Usually full sun is needed to keep the color bright. For evergreens try the genera *Chamaecyparis* and *Juniperus* for rich-gold-leaved cultivars.

Deciduous shrubs include golden alder (*Almus incana* 'Aurea'), golden elder (*Sambucus canadensis* 'Aurea'), golden mock orange (*Philadelphus coronarius* 'Aureus'), golden ninebark (*Physocarpus opulifolius* 'Dart's Gold'), pink-flowering spirea ('Gold Mound'), and a cranberry bush (*Viburnum opulus* 'Xanthocarpum') that has not only yellow twigs but yellow berries as well as yellow leaves. Yellow and golden-leaved shrubs are particularly striking when paired with purple smokebush (*Cotinus* spp.).

DECIDUOUS
Spirea (spy-REE-uh)

Spireas belong to a large genus, but essentially have two different types of flowering habits: some spireas produce umbels of white flowers on woody growth from the previous year, while in other species flowers are distributed along shoots of new wood, the small white blooms appearing on bare branches. *Spiraea thunbergii* is the latter type and is the earliest spirea to bloom. It came originally from China, via Japan, in about 1863. It has autumn foliage color in addition to very early spring bloom. The other type of flowering pattern is characterized by round, umbel-like clusters. Bridal wreath, *Spiraea prunifolia,* has this type of flower in April/May on arching sprays that are also wonderful in flower arrangements. This grows 4–5 feet tall and the shrubs have a fountain shape. From this type many other cultivars have been developed and now there are many shades of pink/red flowers and foliage colors available—for example, S. *japonica* 'Double Play Big Bang', which has bright yellow foliage and large pink flowers on a compact 2–3-foot shrub. These plants are drought-tolerant once established. The native meadowsweet, *Spiraea alba,* has terminal white flower spikes in summer, and requires moist to wet soil. It's best used in naturalistic plantings.

Zones	4–8
Conditions	Full sun; adapts to varied soil types
	Easy to transplant
	Some varieties have repeat blooming
	Fast-growing and durable
Landscape	Used as specimens, foundation plants, hedges, and screening plants
	Propagated by cuttings
	Deer-resistant
	Use for filler in bouquets
Problems	Few problems, no diseases or pests

Baby's Breath Spiraea

Appendix F

Deciduous
Caryopteris (kair-ee-op-ter-iss)
Bluebeard

Caryopteris × *clandonensis* is an Asian import known by the common name of bluebeard. It blooms late August to September and has lovely dense blue flower spikes and neat foliage that and can be used in arrangements. Seed heads form in the fall and persist into winter. These subshrubs are low-growing, drought-tolerant, and magnets for butterflies. Their aromatic foliage makes them unattractive to deer. Since flowers come on the new growth the plants should be pruned back to 10 inches in early spring. This is a low-maintenance subshrub, and there is a variety with bright gold foliage ('Jason') all season long, which contrasts with the amethyst-blue flowers in late summer/early fall. The name Caryopteris derives from its producing winged fruit, as *karyon* means nut and *pteron* means a wing. The hybrid C. × *clandonensis* was an accidental cross appearing in the garden of a Mr. Simmonds in England in 1930. The soft blue flowers are not attention-grabbing at a distance, so they are best planted in intimate spaces or as a line of shrubs edging a path. In shrub borders they are useful in the foreground as foils for more brightly colored, bigger shrubs.

Zones	5–9
Site	Sun, well-drained moist soil
	May be cut to the ground each spring, like a perennial
Height and Spread	3–4'
	Mounding habit
Conditions	Full sun, well-drained humus-rich soil
	Can be propagated by seed or soft-tip cuttings in early summer

Tip: Sometimes not long-lived in zone 5, so site in a protected spot or replant. Periodically flowers on new wood. 'Longwood Blue' is a popular cultivar.

Bluebeard

Appendix G

DECIDUOUS
Cephalanthus (sef-uh-LAN-thus)
Buttonbush

Cephalanthus occidentalis (buttonbush) has globe-shaped inflorescences of small white flowers and grows well in wet limestone or clay-based areas. Butterflies love the nectar, and the shrub serves as a host plant for many species of lepidoptera, including the saddleback caterpillar, the hickory horned devil (royal walnut moth), and caterpillars of the promethea moth and hydrangea sphinx. In the wild buttonbushes like to grow by streams and in swamps, so they need supplemental water in gardens if drought occurs during summer. There are only about six species of shrubs and small trees in this genus. They are native to temperate areas in North America, Asia, and Africa and easily cultivated in fertile soil that provides moisture. Propagate by cuttings of green wood in spring and mature wood in fall. Cephalanthus makes good accents in borders or may be massed. It is a great shrub for a rain garden or swale. It is moderately deer-resistant.

Zones	5–9
Site	Sun to part sun in moisture-retentive soil
	Do not plant on slopes or in raised beds
Pests	No serious pests
Foliage	Leaves are opposite or whorled depending on species

Buttonbush
with Zebra Swallowtail

Appendix H. Dwarf Evergreens

Dry shade	Dry sun
Tsuga canadensis 'Bacon Cristate'	*Abies balsamea* 'Piccolo'
Tsuga canadensis 'Cole's Prostrate'	*Abies koreana* 'Silberperle'
Tsuga canadensis 'Hornbeck'	*Picea glauca* 'Pendula'
Tsuga canadensis 'Jervis'	*Picea pungens* 'Fat Albert'
Tsuga canadensis 'Moon Frost'	*Pinus cembra* 'Stricta'
Fertilize these shrubs in the fall	*Pinus thunbergii* 'Thunderhead'
and water-in well.	*Pinus flexilis* 'Glauca Pendula'
N.B. The aphid-like hemlock woolly	*Pinus contorta* 'Chief Joseph'
adelgid has recently spread to the	*Chamaecyparis nootkatensis* 'Jubilee'
Midwest, posing a threat to	*Chamaecyparis obtusa* 'Fernspray Gold'
Tsuga species.	*Chamaecyparis obtusa* 'Sunny Swirl'
	Chamaecyparis pisifera 'Cream Ball'

INTERESTING FORMS

Ilex crenata 'Sky Pencil' (vertical)
Pieris japonica (airy)
Thuja occidentalis 'Bobazam' (globe)

UNDERPLANTINGS

Groundcovers for dry shade include epimedium, lamium, brunnera, Lenten rose, tiarella, and martagon lilies. *Salix repens* 'Boyd's Pendulous' is a prostrate willow that produces pussy willow buds in early spring. This woody plant grows like a groundcover in zones 4–8 in sun/partial shade and tolerates drought. *Paxistima canbyi* is a 6–12-inch evergreen shrub that can be used as a groundcover in zones 4–9. It tolerates dry and exposed sites. Box huckleberry (*Gaylussacia brachycera*) is a native evergreen groundcover in zones 4–9. It is a heath plant, so it likes damp acid soils.

Groundcovers for dry sun include low-growing varieties of sedum, and *Juniperus horizontalis* 'Wiltonii', a cultivar of the native prostrate or creeping juniper called "blue rug." It adapts to most soil types as long as they are well-drained, and spreads to form a mat that acts as a natural weed barrier. Zones 3–9.

Appendix I. Evergreen Shrubs for Shade

Name	Height	Uses	Conditions
Arborvitae	Up to 20'	Hedges, screen, accents	Bright shade
English boxwood	4–6'	Hedges, foundations	Bright shade
Korean boxwood	1–4'	Clipped formal edgings	Sun/light shade & accents
Shrub holly	4–6'	Hedges, foundations	Bright shade
Oregon grape (fruits)	3–8'	Foundations, slopes	Medium shade
Mountain laurel (flowers)	5–8'	Woodlands, mixed borders	Medium shade
Pieris (flowers)	4–6'	Borders, accents	Medium shade
Yews (may be dense, columnar, or spreading)	Vary according to type	Hedges, accents, screens, foundations	Medium shade

Chokeberry (*Aronia*)	5–8'	Fruit Fall color	Bright shade
Azalea	3–8'	Flowers	Medium shade
Cotoneaster	2–8'	Showy fruit	Bright shade
Dogwood (*Cornus* shrubs)	6–8'	Flowers Fruits	Bright shade
Five-leaf Azalea	6–8'	Barren	Deep shade
Forsythia	6–9'	Early flowers	Bright shade
Fothergilla	3–8'	Flowers	Bright shade
Kerria	4–5'	Flowers	Medium shade
Hydrangea (oakleaf)	4–6'	Flowers	Deep shade
Hypericum	2–4'	Flowers	Bright shade
Mock orange (*Philadelphus*)	3–15'	Flowers	Medium shade
Potentilla	2–4'	Flowers	Medium shade
Spirea	3–6'	Flowers Some foliage color	Bright shade
Clethra	4–6'	Flowers fragrant	Bright shade
Viburnum (many)	4–8'	Flowers Fruits Some foliage color	Bright shade

Appendix K

NATIVE DECIDUOUS
Dwarf *Fothergilla* (foth-uh-GIL-uh)
Witch-alder

Fothergilla gardenii, commonly called witch-alder, is native to the southeastern United States. This dwarf has an upright twiggy habit and grows 2–3 feet tall with similar spread. White fragrant flower spikes resemble pussy willows in April/May as they bloom on naked stems. Flowering stems are excellent for indoor arrangements. It is a trouble-free shrub with three-season interest and seldom needs pruning. The dark green leaves show up well as they turn in the fall into brilliant yellows and oranges. They like acidic soil, so they do well near both needleleaf and broadleaf evergreens. Use them in foundation plantings or shrub borders, or massed in combination with rhododendrons. *F. major* 'Mt. Airy' is a tall, 5–9-foot species that makes an excellent hedge, with dense foliage, upright habit, and prolific flowering. These shrubs do not thrive in wet, alkaline soils. Dwarf *Fothergilla gardenii* 'Blue Mist' is only 24–34 inches tall and 36–48 inches wide. It has blue foliage and honey-scented white bottlebrush blooms in the spring, and the neat rounded shape is a bonus. The frosty blue foliage turns yellow and red in the fall.

Zones	5–9
Site	Full sun to partial shade
	Plant in spring in woodland settings near evergreens to provide acidity
	Tolerant of clay soil
Pests and Diseases	No significant pests or disease
Foliage	Excellent fall color

Autumn leaf of Fothergilla

Appendix L

DECIDUOUS
Lagerstroemia (Lah-ger-STREAM-ee-uh)
Crape Myrtle

Lagerstroemia indica is commonly known as crape (or crepe) myrtle because the flowers have a texture that resembles crepe fabric. The plants originated in southern and eastern Asia, and most are trees that thrive in warm climates. Bloom occurs when few other shrubs are in flower, so crape myrtles can carry the garden during summer heat. Lagerstroemia is useful as a specimen and in hedges and likes good drainage and full sun. The showy flowers have crinkly margins and the individual blooms are massed into large panicles borne at the ends of the branches. The National Arboretum began breeding crape myrtles in the late 1950s (see www.usna.usda.gov), and the first hybrids they developed were introduced in 1978. A 10-feet-tall and -wide shrub, 'Acoma', and the short shrubs 'Pocomoke', 'Hopi', and 'Chickasaw', named for American Indian tribes, came from the program and they are hardy to zone 6 and with protection to zone 5. Leaves can be medium or dark green or bronze. Bloom takes place in August or high summer. They shrug off humidity and are resistant to deer. They are killed to the ground in cold winters but start up again each spring. In southern regions they grow into full-size trees, since they do not experience winter kill. In the southern hemisphere their common name is Christmas bush, as they bloom in December, which is high summer.

Zones	6–11
Conditions	Full sun
	Well-drained humus-rich soil
	Shelter from strong winds
	Propagate from cuttings
	Drought-resistant
	Tolerates dry, poor soil and extreme heat
	Fertilize in winter
Pests and Diseases	No significant pests

Crape Myrtle

Appendix M. Accent Shrubs

Accent Shrubs	Zones	Common Name
Kalmia latifolia 'Sarah'	5–9	Mountain laurel (pink)
Enkianthus campanulatus	4–7	Redvein 　Spring flowers 　Fall foliage
Hamamelis × intermedia	5–9	Hybrid witch-hazel 　Compact 　Blooms late winter
Malus 'Lollizam'	4–7	Dwarf crabapple 　White spring bloom 　Red fall fruit
Ilex glabra 'Shamrock'	4–9	Native evergreen inkberry 　4'
Viburnum dentatum 'Christom'	2–8	Arrowwood viburnum 　Native, 4', berries
Thuja occidentalis 'Fire Chief'	3–7	Dwarf arborvitae 　4' tall & wide 　Red foliage tips 　Rounded shape
Picea alcoquiana 'Howell's Dwarf Tigertail'	3–7	Spruce, grows to 6' 　Tolerant of clay soil
Syringa 'Beauty of Moscow'	3–7	Lilac with white double flowers 　Good scented cut flower
Prunus glandulosa 'Rosea Plena'	5–8	Flowering almond 　Double pink 　Flowers in spring

Appendix N. Invasive Shrubs First Introduced into North America as Ornamentals

Autumn olive (Elaeagnus umbellata)

Russian olive (Elaeagnus angustifolia)

Privet (Lugustrum vulgare)

Multiflora rose (Rosa multiflora)

Asian honeysuckle (Lonicera spp.)

Lantana

Common buckthorn (Rhamnus cathartica)

Japanese barberry (Berberis thunbergii)

Kudzu

Black alder (Alnus glutinosa)

Bicolor/shrubby lespedeza (L. bicolor)

Winged burning bush (Euonymus alatus)

Appendix O. Native Shrubs to Sustain Wildlife

There are many cultivars of shrubs native to the Midwest, but below is a list of some of the "wild-type" species that adapt well to the garden. Where to obtain these plants? There are ever more nurseries devoted to selling natives, and mainstream nurseries that carry at least some native plants. A search on the Web for a particular shrub will reveal sources, and Web sites of native plant societies (such as the Indiana Plant and Wildflower Society at www.inpaws.org, and Wild Ones at www.for-wild.org) list places in the area that sell natives. These societies often host their own plant sales, as do state parks, water and soil conservation districts, and county extension agencies. Membership in native plant organizations will provide the gardener with greater access to natives through plant swaps and plant rescues. Most groups also sponsor tours of native gardens in their community and offer botanical walks that allow the gardener to see plants in their native habitats.

Species	Benefits	Larval species hosted
American hazelnut (*Corylus americana*)	Nuts and catkins for wildlife	polyphemus moth
Chokeberry (*Aronia* spp.)	Flowers provide nectar, fruit for wildlife	coral hairstreak butterfly
Blueberry/huckleberry (*Vaccinium* spp.)	Flowers provide nectar, fruits for wildlife	striped hairstreak, Henry's elfin, and spring azure butterflies, huckleberry sphinx moth
Buttonbush (*Cephalanthus occidentalis*)	Flowers provide food for insects and hummingbirds, seeds for wildlife	Saddleback caterpillar, hickory horned devil, promethea moth, hydrangea sphinx moth
Dogwood (*Cornus* spp.)	Flowers provide nectar, fruit for wildlife	spring azure butterfly, polyphemus moth
New Jersey tea (*Ceanothus americanus*)	Flowers provide food for insects and hummingbirds, seeds for wildlife	Various moths
Serviceberry (*Amelanchier arborea* or *laevis*)	Flowers provide early source of nectar, early fruit for breeding birds	striped hairstreak, viceroy, and red-spotted purple butterflies
Spicebush (*Lindera benzoin*)	Flowers provide early source of nectar, fruits for wildlife	spicebush swallowtail and promethea moth
Sumac (*Rhus* spp.)	Flowers provide nectar, persistent fruits for wildlife	showy emerald moth, hickory horned devil

Species	Benefits	Larval species hosted
Sweet pepper bush (*Clethra alnifolia*)	Flowers provide nectar for insects and hummingbirds, fruit for wildlife	various moths
Viburnum (*Viburnum* spp.)	Flowers provide nectar, fruit for wildlife	spring azure butterflies, hummingbird clearwing moths
Winterberry (*Ilex verticillata*)	Nectar for insects, persistent fruit for wildlife	Harris' three-spot moth

OTHER NATIVE SHRUBS TO GROW IN THE MIDWESTERN GARDEN:

American beautyberry (*Callicarpa americana*)
Common ninebark (*Physocarpus opulifolius*)
Common snowberry (*Symphoricarpos albus*)
Coralberry (*Symphoricarpos orbiculatus*)
Juniper (*Juniperus communis*)
Leatherwood (*Dirca pallustris*)
Mock orange (*Philadelphus inodorus*)
Mountain laurel (*Kalmia latifolia*)
Sweet shrub/Carolina allspice (*Calycanthus floridus*)
Virginia sweetspire (*Itea virginica*)
Wahoo (*Euonymous atropurpureus*)
White meadowsweet (*Spiraea alba*)
Witch-alder (*Fothergilla*)
Witch-hazel (*Hamamalis virginiana* or *vernalis*)

Brown Thrasher

Appendix P. Plants That Seem Unappetizing to Deer

NOTE

Deer will eat anything if hungry enough, and this is affected by the local deer population and the weather. A high fence is the best deterrent. Repellents that include putrescent egg solids, ammonium soaps of fatty acids, or capsaicin work best. Mixing cayenne pepper with birdseed deters deer, but not the birds. Deer damage is obvious when flower heads are missing, stems look broken, or plants are pulled up entirely or eaten to the ground.

Plant deer-resistant perennials at the base of shrubs.

Botanical Name	Common Name
Allium spp.	Ornamental chive/onion
Epimedium spp.	Epimedium
Achillea spp.	Yarrow
Ilex opaca	American holly (shrub)
Buxus sempervirens	Boxwood (shrub)
Begonia spp.	Begonia
Tropaeolum majus	Nasturtium
Galium odoratum	Sweet woodruff
Pulmonaria spp.	Lungwort
Osmunda cinnamomea	Cinnamon fern
Echinacea purpurea	Purple coneflower
Digitalis spp.	Foxglove
Dicentra spectabilis	Bleeding heart
Heuchera spp.	Coral bells
Helleborus orientalis	Lenten rose
Perovskia	Russian sage
Viburnum prunifolium	Black haw (shrub)
Amelanchier spp.	Serviceberry (shrub or small tree)
Lindera benzoin	Spicebush
Cephalanthus occidentalis	Buttonbush

Appendix Q. Shrubs for Cut Flowers

Hydrangea
Bluebeard (*Caryopteris*)
Flowering quince (*Chaenomeles*)
Scotch broom (*Cytisus*)
European cornel (*Cornus mas*)
Deutzia
Witch-alder (*Fothergilla*)
Mountain laurel (*Kalmia latifolia*)
Azalea
Rhododendron

Forsythia
Witch-hazel (*Hamamelis*)
Mock orange (*Philadelphus*)
Flowering almond (*Prunus*)
Willow (*Salix*)
Meadowsweet (*Spiraea*)
Lilac (*Syringa*)
Weigela
Chasteberry (*Vitex*)

Appendix R. Tall Native Perennials

(Use as companions for shrubs.)

Wild indigo (*Baptisia australis*) produces spectacular spires of blue pea-type flowers in May. It grows to 4 feet and does not need staking. It is hardy to zone 4 and prefers sun and average moisture. *Baptisia* is long-lived and difficult to move. It has black seedpods that can be useful for flower arrangers, and it will self-seed if in an unmulched bed or berm.

Queen of the prairie (*Filipendula rubra*) produces feathery pink flower heads in June that are similar to astilbes, and grows 5–7 feet but does not need staking. It needs moisture-retentive soil and can form large colonies if planted in an appropriate site, i.e., one with even moisture, and with sun but some shade in the hottest part of the day to avoid leaves scorching. The shrub can be cut back to encourage new growth of the handsome foliage. It is hardy to zones 3–8.

Foxglove beardtongue (*Penstemon digitalis*) is the most moisture-tolerant of the penstemon species and likes dry soils in full sun to light shade. White or pink flowers appear in May and attract bees and hummingbirds. It is hardy to zone 3 and grows 3–4 feet. A good cultivar is 'Husker Red'.

Butterfly weed (*Asclepias tuberosa*) is a prairie plant, so it enjoys dry soil. It is one of the two native milkweeds that adapt best to cultivation. Monarch caterpillars feed on the leaves and adult monarchs like the nectar. It grows to 3 feet in full sun with bright orange flowers, and it has a tap root so it does not like to be moved. Since it has tuberous (fleshy) roots that penetrate deep into the soil, it can sustain itself during drought. It has a typical milkweed pod with silky seeds that fly well in the wind, so capture some of the seeds and bury them elsewhere in your garden to grow new plants. A new pink variety is also available. There is also a tall swamp milkweed (*A. incarnata*) that grows to 4 feet and enjoys moisture and thus likes clay, as it is moisture-retentive. It does not have a tap root and so can easily be moved. All milkweed seem to attract yellow aphids in July/August in our Midwest gardens. Use a hose to wash them off.

Flowering spurge (*Euphorbia corollata*) looks like baby's breath when it blooms in July/August in the garden. It will grow in dry or moist soils in zones 5–8 and is 3 feet tall.

Cardinal flower and blue lobelia (*Lobelia cardinalis* and *L. siphilitica*) are moisture-loving prairie plants that will grow in home gardens in part shade. They grow 3–4 feet high with a spire of flowers in late summer. They are reseeding, short-lived perennials, and they attract hummingbirds. They will set a rosette of leaves at first and then set the tall flower spike late in the summer. Other prairie plants that are good garden specimens are purple coneflower (*Echinacea*), blazing star (*Liatris*), and aster (*Symphyotrichum novae-angliae*), in both tall and short varieties.

Woodland aster (*Eurybia divaricata*) grows to about 2–3 feet in my garden and self-seeds a lot, popping up all over. Use it as filler in flower arrangements like a coarse baby's breath. Blooms in September/October when other perennials are finished. There are other, similar species (e.g., *Symphyotrichum lateriflorum*).

Bugbane (*Cimicifuga racemosa*) is a tall, 4–8 foot perennial with tall white flower spires in late summer. It grows in zones 3–6 and likes even moisture in sun to part shade.

NATIVE WILDFLOWERS
(PLANT IN SHADE UNDER DECIDUOUS TREES AND SHRUBS):

Bloodroot (*Sanguinaria canadensis*)
Rue anemone (*Thalictrum thalictroides*)
False rue anemone (*Enemion biternatum*)
Spring beauty (*Claytonia virginica*)
Dutchman's breeches (*Dicentra cucullaria*)
Squirrel corn (*Dicentra canadensis*)
Virginia bluebells (*Mertensia virginica*)
Wild ginger (*Asarum canadense*)
Jack-in-the-Pulpit (*Arisaema triphyllum*)
Trillium spp.

Monarch caterpillar on Butterfly weed

Appendix S

Deciduous

Aesculus (EASE-cull-is)

Bottlebrush buckeye

Aesculus parviflora, the bottlebrush buckeye, is a suckering shrub that can grow over 10 feet tall and infinitely wide. It blooms in June and July with upright white spikes and is hardy to zone 5. The individual racemes of white flowers have filaments tipped with pale pink anthers. The compound leaves have five to seven little leaflets. It blooms in midsummer and then fruits. Plant in early spring in moist, humus-rich soil in full sun to light shade.

Zones	4–8
Site	Provide good air circulation to avoid fungal diseases such as leaf blotch and canker.
	Plant in spring
Pests and Diseases	Japanese beetles eat leaves
Landscape Uses	Excellent specimen shrub for a large area. Can also be used on banks that are difficult to mow, or as a hedge. Can also edge a wooded area. May be trained as a single trunk to form a small tree

Fruit of Bottlebrush Buckeye

References

Barnes, B., and W. Wagner, Jr. 1981. *Michigan trees: A guide to the trees of Michigan and the Great Lakes region.* Ann Arbor: University of Michigan Press.

Brown, J. 1999. *The pursuit of paradise.* Glasgow: Omnia Books.

Cullina, W. 2002. *Native trees, shrubs, and vines.* Boston: Houghton Mifflin.

Darke, R. 2002. *The American woodland garden: Capturing the spirit of the deciduous forest.* Portland, Ore.: Timber Press.

Dirr, M. 1998. *Manual of woody landscape plants.* 5th ed. Champaign, Ill.: Stipes.

Gleason, H., and A. Cronquist. 1991. *Manual of vascular plants of northeastern United States and adjacent Canada.* 2nd ed. Bronx: New York Botanical Garden Press.

Gribbin, M., and J. Gribbin. 2008. *Flower hunters.* New York: Oxford University Press.

Lady Bird Johnson Wildflower Center, The University of Texas at Austin. www.wildflower.org. Accessed June 16, 2012.

Missouri Botanical Garden. www.missouribotanicalgarden.org. Accessed June 16, 2012.

Neal, B. 1992. *Gardener's Latin.* Chapel Hill, N.C.: Algonquin Books.

Spry, C. 1962. *How to do the flowers.* London: Dent.

Staff of the L. H. Bailey Hortorium, Cornell University. 1976. *Hortus third: A concise dictionary of plants cultivated in the United States and Canada.* New York: McMillian.

Stewart, A. 2007. *Flower confidential: The good, the bad, and the beautiful in the business of flowers.* Chapel Hill, N.C.: Algonquin Books.

Stokes, D., and L. Stokes. 1998. *Stokes bird gardening book: The complete guide to creating a bird-friendly habitat in your backyard.* Boston: Little, Brown.

Tallamy, D. W. 2009. *Bringing nature home: How you can sustain wildlife with native plants.* Rev. ed. Portland, Ore.: Timber Press.

USDA Plants Database. http://plants.usda.gov. Accessed June 16, 2012.

Wagner, D. 2005. *Caterpillars of Eastern North America: A guide to identification and natural history.* Princeton: Princeton University Press.

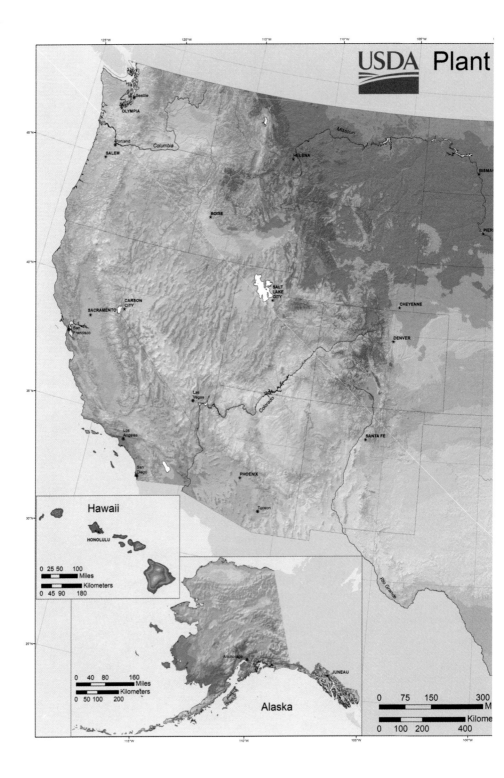

Hardiness Zone Map

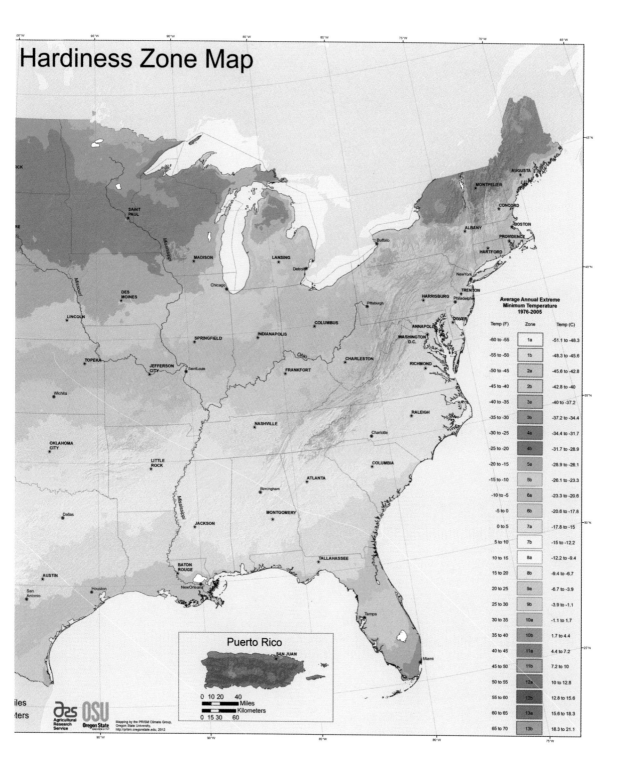

Average Annual Extreme
Minimum Temperature
1976-2005

Temp (F)	Zone	Temp (C)
-60 to -55	1a	-51.1 to -48.3
-55 to -50	1b	-48.3 to -45.6
-50 to -45	2a	-45.6 to -42.8
-45 to -40	2b	-42.8 to -40
-40 to -35	3a	-40 to -37.2
-35 to -30	3b	-37.2 to -34.4
-30 to -25	4a	-34.4 to -31.7
-25 to -20	4b	-31.7 to -28.9
-20 to -15	5a	-28.9 to -26.1
-15 to -10	5b	-26.1 to -23.3
-10 to -5	6a	-23.3 to -20.6
-5 to 0	6b	-20.6 to -17.8
0 to 5	7a	-17.8 to -15
5 to 10	7b	-15 to -12.2
10 to 15	8a	-12.2 to -9.4
15 to 20	8b	-9.4 to -6.7
20 to 25	9a	-6.7 to -3.9
25 to 30	9b	-3.9 to -1.1
30 to 35	10a	-1.1 to 1.7
35 to 40	10b	1.7 to 4.4
40 to 45	11a	4.4 to 7.2
45 to 50	11b	7.2 to 10
50 to 55	12a	10 to 12.8
55 to 60	12b	12.8 to 15.6
60 to 65	13a	15.6 to 18.3
65 to 70	13b	18.3 to 21.1

Puerto Rico

SAN JUAN

0 10 20 40
Miles
Kilometers
0 15 30 60

Miles
eters

Agricultural
Research
Service

Oregon State
UNIVERSITY

Mapping by the PRISM Climate Group,
Oregon State University.
http://prism.oregonstate.edu, 2012

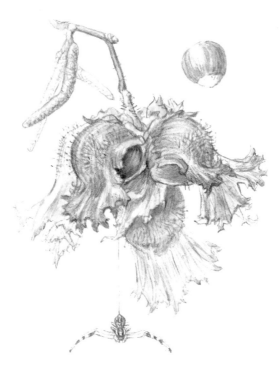

Ripening Hazelnuts
and Running Crab Spider

Index

Italicized page numbers refer to illustrations. Page numbers followed by t indicate a table.

Abelia: A. mosanensis, 10, 16t; glossy abelia (*Abelia* × *grandiflora*), 16t; pruning of, 115; and wildlife, 53
Abies koreana 'Aurea' (fir), 37
abutilon, 17
accent shrubs, xii, 118, 127
Acer japonicum 'Dissectum' (cutleaf maple), 11
acid-loving shrubs in alkaline soils, 6
Aesculus parviflora (bottlebrush buckeye), 26–27, 47, 134
Agastache rupestris (Hummingbird hyssop), 30
'Alba' (*V. agnus-castus*), 105
Alberta spruce, 113
alders, 36, 37, 53
alkaline soils, acid-loving shrubs in, 6
alliums, 67
Alnus incana 'Aurea', 30
althea. *See* rose of Sharon
amaranth, 68
Amelanchier. See serviceberries
American beautyberry (*Callicarpa americana*), 106, 107; in hedgerows, 37; and wildlife, 52t, 53. *See also* beautyberry
American flowering dogwood (*Cornus florida*), 49
American hazelnuts (*Corylus americana*), 37
amsonia, 35
'Annabelle' (*Hydrangea arborescens*), 17, 28
aphids, 43
'Arborea' (*Hamamelis japonica*), 25
arborvitae, 15
Arisaemas, 32
'Arnold Promise' witch-hazel, 109
Aronia. See chokeberries
arrangements of flowers, 56–70; characteristics of, 63–65; containers for, 58; dried arrangements, 69; easy arrangement ideas, 61–63; forcing branches, 56–57; guidelines for, 60–61; historical perspective on,

57–58; by month, 65–69; shrubs for, 131; supports for, 58–60
arrowwood (*Viburnum dentatum*), 46, 79
Aruncus dioicus (Goatsbeard variety), 31
Asclepias incarnata (swamp milkweed), 31
Asclepias tuberosa (butterfly weed), 28, 67
Asian bittersweet, 45
Asian honeysuckle, 45
Asiatic garden beetles, 51
asters, 49, 68
astilbes, 68
'Athens' (*Calycanthus floridus*), 101
'Aurea' (*Abies koreana*), 37
'Aurea' (*Alnus incana*), 30
autumn-blooming witch-hazel (*Hamamelis virginiana*), 10, 108, 109
'Autumn Brilliance' (*Amelanchier*), 22
autumn olive, 45
'Avalanche' (*Pieris japonica*), 77
azalea lace bugs, 46
azaleas: in arrangements, 60; and early plant explorers, 50; pruning of, 115; requirements of, 25; sites for, 4, 12

baby's breath, 67
'Baileyi' (*Cornus*), 87
banks in sunny sites, 26
baptisia, 66
Barberry (*Berberis*), 115
basil, 68
beach plum (*Prunus maritima*), 27
beautyberry (*Callicarpa*), 106, 107; American beautyberry (*C. americana*), 37, 52t, 53, 106, 107; in arrangements, 62, 68; *C. japonica*, 107; colors of, 3, 107; 'Early Amethyst' (*C. dichotoma*), 107; foliage and fruit of, 3, 35; fruit of, 35, 52t, 106, 107; in hedgerows, 37; in mixed-shrub berms, 25; pruning of, 115; and wildlife, 46, 52t, 53

beauty bush, 53
beebalm (*Monarda didyma*), 30–31
beech, 69
bees, 41–42, 53
Berberis (Barberry), 115
berms, 23–24, 25–26
berries, 52t. *See also* fruiting shrubs
biodiversity, 44–46, 50
birds, 34–37; benefits of shrubs for, 2; bird seed and feeders, 35–36, 38; and fruiting shrubs, 51–53, 52t; migrations of, 53; nest-building of, 38; and nonnative shrubs, 45; predation on insects of, 35, 36, 37
blackberries (*Rubus* genus), 36, 37, 52t
black chokeberries (*Aronia melanocarpa*), 52t, 82
black-eyed Susans, 67
black haw (*Viburnum prunifolium*), 78, 79
'Black Lace' (*Sambucus nigra*), 26, 36
'Bloomerang' lilac, 85
blooming shrubs. *See* flowering shrubs
Bluebeard (*Caryopteris*), 16t, 115, 120
blueberries (*Vaccinium*): advantages of, 48; fruit of, 52; soil type requirements of, 6; as substitute for invasive species, 46; and wildlife, 35, 36, 52t
'Blue Bird' rose of Sharon, 31
blue lobelia (*Lobelia siphilitica*), 31
blue spruce, 66, 67, 112
borders, 15–18
bottlebrush buckeye (*Aesculus parviflora*), 26–27, 47, 134
boxwoods, 112; applications of, 47–48; in arrangements, 66, 67; and deer, 15, 47; English boxwood, 17; foliage of, 9, 113; in foundational plantings, 21; in hedges and borders, 13, 14, 15, 17; planting guidelines for, 21; pruning of, 21; roots of, 15; in topiaries, 17; 'Vardar Valley' (*Buxus sempervirens*), 37
'Brandywine' (*Viburnum nudum*), 79

'Bridal Wreath' spirea, 66
'Brilliantissima' chokeberries, 83
'Britt-Marie Crawford' (*Ligularia dentata*), 32
broom (*Cytisus* spp.): in arrangements, 62; 'Hollandia' (*Cytisus* × *praecox*), 39–40; on slopes, 27
'Brouwer's Beauty' (*Pieris floribunda* × *japonica*), 77
buckeye (also known as bottlebrush), 26–27, 47
Buddleia (butterfly bush), 35, 45, 115
bumblebees, 42
burning bush (*Euonymus alatus*), 22, 46
butterflies, 41, 45
butterfly bush (*Buddleia*), 35, 45, 115
butterfly weed (*Asclepias*), 28, 67
buttonbush (*Cephalanthus occidentalis*), 121; features of, 10; and insects, 45–46; sites for, 4; and wildlife, 53
Buxus sempervirens 'Vardar Valley', 37

California sweetshrub (*Calycanthus occidentalis*), 101
Calycanthus, 66, 100, 101
camellia, 50, 69
'Cameo' (*Chaenomelis* × *superba*), 36
Cardinal flower (*Lobelia cardinalis*), 31
Carex bromoides, 31
Carex nigra, 31
'Carnea' (*Hamamelis vernalis*), 25
Carolina Allspice (*Calycanthus floridus*), 100, 101
'Carol Mackie' daphne, 67
Caryopteris: in arrangements, 62, 66, 68; bluebeard, 16t, 115, 120; 'First Choice,' 16t; in mixed-shrub berms, 25; pruning of, 115; 'Sunshine Blue', 16t
caterpillars: food sources of, 42, 44; and fruiting shrubs, 53; promethea moth caterpillar, 46; spicebush swallowtail caterpillars, 37, 45, 73
Catesby, Mark, 101
Catmint (*Nepeta* spp.), 29, 66
Ceanothus americanus (New Jersey tea), 12
Cephalanthus occidentalis. See buttonbush
Cephalotaxus harringtonia (Japanese plum yew), 10
Ceratostigma plumbaginoides (plumbago), 22
Cercis, 115
Chaenomeles. See flowering quince

Chamaecyparis obtusa 'Fernspray Gold', 37
'Chardonnay Pearls' (*Deutzia gracilis*), 16t
chasteberry, 115
chaste tree (*Vitex agnus-castus*), 104, 105
Chelone: *C. glabra*, 31; *C. lyonii*, 31; *C. obliqua*, 31
chokeberries (*Aronia*), 82, 83; black chokeberries (*Aronia melanocarpa*), 52t, 82; 'Brilliantissima', 83; red chokeberries (*Aronia arbutifolia*), 52t, 82; seasonal considerations for, 116; and wildlife, 35, 46, 52t
chrysanthemums, 50, 68
cinnamon fern (*Osmundastrum cinnamomeum*), 31
clematis: as mock orange companion, 93; and supports in arrangements, 59
Clethra. See sweet pepper bush
'Codsall Pink' (*Deutzia scabra*), 11, 16t
colonial era, 48–49
color considerations in plant selection, 18–19
'Compacta' (*Viburnum carlesii*), 79
compact varieties of shrubs, 3
composition principles, 19
compost, 6
coneflowers, 62
'Conica' (*Pica glauca*), 113
conifers: in arrangements, 63; foliage of, 113; sites for, 28; for small gardens, 117
Cornus. See dogwoods
Corylus. See hazelnut
Cotinus (smoke bush), 11, 17, 25
Cotoneaster, 17, 21–22, 24
crabapples, 62
crape myrtle: and alien pests, 51; in arrangements, 68; blooming habits of, 35; *Lagerstroemia indica*, 126; in mixed-shrub berms, 25; pruning of, 17, 115; sites for, 4
creeping evergreen junipers, 22
creeping needle evergreens, 26
Creeping phlox (*Phlox subulata*), 26, 29
Cryptomeria japonica 'Knaptonensis' (dwarf Japanese cedar), 11, 37–38
Culinary sage (*Salvia officinalis*), 29
cutleaf maple (*Acer japonicum* 'Dissectum'), 11
cypress hedges, 13
Cytisus. See broom

daffodils, 4, 57, 65, 66
damselflies, 43
daphne: in arrangements, 66, 67; 'Carol Mackie', 67; pruning of, 115; seasonal considerations for, 116; 'Somerset', 25
deciduous shrubs: in borders, 17; in espalier, 17; in hedges, 16t; portion of garden devoted to, 9; shade-tolerant deciduous shrubs, 124; for small gardens, 117; and wildlife, 34, 37
deer: deer-resistant plants, 10, 11, 25, 130; deer-vulnerable plants, 28; and hedges, 15
definition of shrubs, 2
Deutzia: 'Chardonnay Pearls' (*D. gracilis*), 16t; 'Codsall Pink' (*D. scabra*), 11, 16t; pruning of, 115
'Diana' rose of Sharon, 26
Dianthus spp. (Pinks), 29
dill, 68
'Dissectum' (*Acer japonicum*, cutleaf maple), 11
dogwoods (*Cornus*), 86, 87–88; American flowering dogwood (*C. florida*), 49; in arrangements, 62, 66; in hedgerows, 37; kousa dogwood (*C. kousa*), 49, 87; in mixed-shrub berms, 25; red osier dogwoods (*C. sericea*), 86, 87; roughleaf dogwood (*C. drummondii*), 87; roundleaf dogwood (*C. rugosa*), 87; seasonal considerations for, 116; 'Sibirica' (*C. alba*), 116; silky dogwoods (*C. amomum*), 4, 86, 87; sites for, 4; and wildlife, 35, 36, 37, 52t
dragonflies, 43
dried arrangements, 69
dwarf golden arborvitae (*Thuja orientalis*), 113
dwarf Japanese cedar (*Cryptomeria japonica* 'Knaptonensis'), 11
dwarf shrubs: dwarf evergreens, 28; in foundational plantings, 20; in hedges, 15; identifying, on plant tags, 3; maintenance of, 28

'Early Amethyst' (*C. dichotoma*), 107
earthworms, 43
Echinacea, 28
ecodesigners, 59
edging, 21
elderberries (*Sambucus*): 'Black Lace' (*S. nigra*), 26, 36; in hedgerows, 37; and wildlife, 35, 36, 46, 52t

'Elegantissima' (*Gleditsia triacanthos*), 27

Eleutherococcus sieboldiamus 'Variegatus' (fiveleaf aralia), 10

English boxwood, 17

English gardens, 49

espalier, 17

euonymus: burning bush (*E. alatus*), 22, 46; invasive species of, 22, 46; native species of, 46; strawberry bush (*E. americanus*), 53; Wahoo (*E. atropurpureus*), 46, 53

Eupatorium fistulosum (Joe-Pye weed), 30

evergreen shrubs, 2–3, *112, 113*; in arrangements, 62, 63, 67, 69; in borders, 17; broadleaf evergreens, 5, 6, 25, 63, 113; color considerations in, 18–19; creeping needle evergreens, 26; dwarf evergreens, 28, 122; in espalier, 17; foliage of, 113; in foundational plantings, 19; in hedges, 9, 14, 16t, 17; needleleaf evergreens, 25; placement of, 9; planting, 5, 6; portion of garden devoted to, 9; repetition of, in garden design, 113; shade-tolerant evergreens, 11, 123; on slopes, 26–27; for small gardens, 24, 117; in topiaries, 17; and wildlife, 34, 37

Exochorda (Snow Day), 26

exposure considerations, 12

false cypress, 37

'Farrow' Arctic Fire (*Cornus sericea*), 87

ferns, 62, 68

'Fernspray Gold' (*Chamaecyparis obtusa*), 37

fertilizer, 6, 27, 48

fetterbush (*Pieris floribunda*), 77

Filipendula. See meadowsweet

fiveleaf aralia, 10, 16t

flowering almond, 35, 60, 66

flowering plum, 66

flowering quince (*Chaenomeles*), 80, 81; in arrangements, 60, 62, 65, 66; 'Cameo', 36; 'Orange Storm', 81; 'Pink Storm', 81; pruning of, 115; sites for, 4; on slopes, 27; 'Toyo Nishiki', 27, 81; and wildlife, 35, 53

flowering shrubs: in borders, 16; deciduous flowering shrubs, 17; late bloomers, 29–30; and pruning practices, 27; and sites for planting

shrubs, 9; and wildlife, 45; and year-round color, 3. *See also* arrangements of flowers

forcing branches for arrangements, 56–57

forget-me-not (*Myosotis palustris*), 31

forsythia: in arrangements, 62, 65, 66; blooming habits of, 17; dwarf version of, 11; and early plant explorers, 50; pruning of, 115; seasonal considerations for, xii

Fortune, Robert, 50, 91

Fothergilla, 6, 125

foundational plantings, 17, 18–22

Franklinia, 115

frogs (arrangement supports), 58, 63

fruiting shrubs, 36, 48, 51–53, 52t

Gleditsia triacanthos 'Elegantissima', 27

glossy abelia (*Abelia × grandiflora*), 16t

goal setting, 12–13

Goatsbeard varieties, 31

Golden alder (*Alnus incana* 'Aurea'), 30

gold lace juniper, *112*

gooseberries (*Ribes*), 36, 52, 52t

'Grandiflora' (*Hydrangea paniculata*), 11

Great blue lobelia (*Lobelia siphilitica*), 31

green dragon (*Arisaemas dracontium*), 32

Gribbin, J., 50

Gribbin, M., 50

'Gro-Low' (*Rhus aromatica*), 97

groundcovers, 22

groupings of plants, xii, 23–24, 36

grubs, 51

Hamamelis. See witch-hazel

harmony in the garden, 19–20

Harry Lauder's Walking Stick (*Corylus contorta*), 25, 116

hazelnut (*Corylus*): American hazelnuts (*C. americana*), 37; Harry Lauder's Walking Stick (*C. contorta*), 25, 116; seasonal considerations for, 116; and wildlife, 37, 46

hedgerows, 37–38

hedges, 13–15; evergreen hedges, 9, 14, 16t, 17; installation of, 15; maintenance of, 14–15; plant choices for, 14, 15, 16t; uses of, 13–14; and wildlife, 34

height of shrubs, 2

helianthus, 67

hellebore, 66

hemlocks: in arrangements, 67; foliage of, 9; in hedges and borders, 15, 17; hemlock woolly adelgid, 46, 51; sites for, 28; in topiaries, 17; *Tsuga*, 16t

Henry, Mary, 99

'Henry's Garnet' (*Itea virginica*), 3, 48, 98, 99

hibiscus: and alien pests, 51; in borders, 17; pruning of, 115; rose mallow (*Hibiscus moscheutos*), 30; 'Southern Belle', 35; and wildlife, 35, 53

hickory horned devil, 46

highbush cranberry (*Viburnum trilobum*), 37, 79

'Hollandia' (*Cytisus × praecox*), 39–40

hollies, *112*; in arrangements, 68, 69; and boxwoods, 48; in hedges and borders, 13, 17; in mixed-shrub berms, 26; requirements of, 25; seasonal considerations for, 116; in topiaries, 17; and wildlife, 35, 36; winterberry hollies, 26

honeybees, 41–42

honeysuckle, 115

hosta, 61, 68

humilis (shorter than typical) shrubs, 3

Hummingbird hyssop (*Agastache rupestris*), 30

hummingbirds, 23, 41, 53

hybrids, 39–40

hydrangeas: 'Annabelle' (*H. arborescens*), 17, 28; in arrangements, 61–62, 67, 68; and deer, 28; 'Grandiflora' (*H. paniculata*), 11; *H. paniculata*, 68; maintenance of, 28; oakleaf hydrangea (*H. quercifolia*), 11, 28, 67; pruning of, 17; shade-tolerance of, 11; sites for, 4, 12; 'Snow Queen' (*H. quercifolia*), 28; and supports in arrangements, 59; watering needs of, 28; wild hydrangea (*H. arborescens*), 11

Hypericum, 115

'Ice Follies' (daffodils), 57

Ilex species: 'Blue Boy', 16t; and boxwoods, 48; 'Castle Spire' (*Ilex × meservae*), 16t; 'Castle Wall' (*Ilex × meservae*), 16t; Evergreen hollies, 52t; fruits of, 35, 52; *I. serrata*, 52; 'Sky Pencil' (*I. crenata*), 36, 116; and wildlife, 36, 46, 52t. *See also* winterberry

impatiens, 68
imported plants, 48–49
Impressionist painters, 58
Indigofera, 115
insecticides, 46
insects: alien pests, 46, 51; beneficial
    insects, 43; birds' predation on,
    35, 36, 37; and fruiting shrubs, 53;
    metamorphosis of, 42; and native/
    nonnative shrubs, 44–46; and pol-
    lination process, 40–43
invasive species, xi–xii, 44–45, 46, 127
iris, 66, 67
Ironweed varieties, 30
island beds, 23
Itea, 98, 99; in arrangements, 66; and
    boxwoods, 48; 'Henry's Garnet'
    (*I. virginica*), 3, 48, 98, 99; 'Little
    Henry' (*I. virginica*), 99; and sup-
    ports in arrangements, 59; Virginia
    Sweetspire (*I. virginica*), 99
ivy, 69

Jack-in-the-pulpit (*Arisaemas triphyl-
    lum*), 32
Japanese anemones, 50
Japanese aucuba, 11
Japanese beetles, 46, 51
Japanese culture, 63–64, 91
Japanese imports, 49
Japanese mahonia, 50
Japanese maple, 66
Japanese pachysandra (*P. terminalis*),
    49–50
Japanese yews: in hedges and borders,
    17; Japanese plum yew (*Cephalotax-
    us harringtonia*), 10; in topiaries, 17
'Jean's Dilly' (*Picea glauca*), 37
Jensen, Jens, 48
'Jim Dandy' winterberry, 52
Joe-Pye weed (*Eupatorium fistulosum*),
    30
'Josee' lilacs, 85
juncos, 34
junipers: fruit of, 52; gold lace juniper,
    112; in hedges, 15; roots of, 15;
    weeping blue juniper, 112; and
    wildlife, 35
Juniperus, 37

Kalmea latifolia 'Sarah', 116
Kerria, 11, 17, 115
'Knaptonensis' (*Cryptomeria japonica*),
    11, 37–38
Knock Out roses, 3
knot gardens, 13

Korean imports, 49
Korean lilac 'Miss Kim', 66, 84, 85
kousa dogwood (*Cornus kousa*), 49

ladybird beetles, 43
Lagerstroemia indica. See crape myrtle
lamb's ears, 61, 67, 68
lasagna bed preparation, 24
'Latifolia' (*V. agnus-castus*), 105
laurels, 13, 66, 69. *See also* mountain
    laurel
lavender: in arrangements, 66, 67;
    pruning of, 115; sites for, 12
layering plants, 23–24
leaves, raking, 38
Lespedeza, 115
Liatris spicata (Marsh blazing star), 30
light conditions, 8
Ligularia, 32; ligularia leaves, 67
lilacs, 84, 85; in arrangements, 66;
    'Bloomerang', 85; in hedgerows, 37;
    'Josee', 85; 'Miss Canada', 85; 'Miss
    Kim', 66, 84, 85; pruning of, 115;
    sites for, 15, 26; and wildlife, 35
lilies, 67
Lily-of-the-Valley bush (*Pieris ja-
    ponica*), 76, 77; in arrangements, 66;
    'Avalanche', 77; 'Brouwer's Beauty',
    77; *P. floribunda*, 77; requirements
    of, 25; 'Valley Rose', 76; 'Valley
    Valentine', 77
Lindera benzoin (spicebush), 45, 73. *See
    also* spicebush (*L. benzoin*)
Linnaeus, Carl, 47
Liriope, 22
'Little Devil' (*Physocarpus opulifolius*),
    95
littleleaf cotoneaster (*C. microphyl-
    lus*), 24
Lobelia: *L. cardinalis* (Cardinal flower),
    31; *L. siphilitica* (blue lobelia), 31
low-growing shrubs, 3

magnolias: in arrangements, 62, 66, 69;
    and early plant explorers, 50; prun-
    ing of, 115; saucer magnolia tree, 62;
    star magnolia (*M. stellata*), 11
Mahonias (*Mahonia*): in arrangements,
    68; *M. aquifolium*, 49; *M. bealei*, 49;
    M. japonica, 49; and wildlife, 52t
maintenance requirements of shrubs,
    3, 27–28
Mallow (*Malva fastigiata*), 30
malva, 30, 68
Marsh blazing star (*Liatris spicata*), 30
mazes, 14

McMahon, Bernard, 49
meadowsweet (*Filipendula*): in
    arrangements, 67; *F. palmata*, 31;
    F. purpurea, 31; *F. ulmaria*, 31;
    pruning of, 115; sites for, 31
Menzies, 49
Michigan holly, 111
'Minnesota Snowflake' (*P.* × *virginalis*),
    93
mint, 67, 68
'Miss Canada' lilacs, 85
'Miss Kim' lilacs, 66, 84, 85
Mitchell, John, 47
Mitchella repens (partridge berry),
    46–47
mockingbirds, 34
mock orange (*Philadelphus inodorous*),
    92, 93; in arrangements, 60, 62,
    66; in hedgerows, 37; 'Minnesota
    Snowflake' (*P.* × *virginalis*), 93;
    pruning of, 115
moisture loving plants, 30–32
monarda, 30–31, 67
mountain laurel: in arrangements, 60;
    and *Pieris japonica,* 77; requirements
    of, 25; seasonal considerations for,
    116
mowing strip, 21
'Mt. Airy' (*Fothergilla*), 6
mulch, 6, 21
multiflora roses, 45
mums, 68
Myosotis palustris (forget-me-not), 31
myrtles, 13

nannyberry (*Viburnum lentago*), 79
native shrubs, 44–48; definition of, xii,
    44; early advocates of, 48; historical
    perspective on, 48–50; pest-vulnera-
    bilities of, 10; sites for, 5, 10; unusual
    natives, 10–12; and wildlife, 10
nectar, 40–41, 45–46, 53
Nepeta spp. (Catmint), 29
New Jersey tea (*Ceanothus americanus*),
    12, 36, 53
ninebark (*Physocarpus*), 94, 95; in
    arrangements, 66; in hedgerows, 37;
    'Little Devil' (*P. opulifolius*), 95
nomenclature, 39
nonnative shrubs, 44–50
nursery tags on plants, 3

oakleaf hydrangea (*H. quercifolia*), 11,
    28, 67
Oasis arrangement foam, 59, 61
opal basil, 61, 67, 68

'Orange Storm' (*Chaenomeles*), 81
Oregon holly-grape, 49
Oriental beetles, 51
Osmunda regalis (royal fern), 31
Osmundastrum cinnamomeum (cinnamon fern), 31
Ozark witch-hazel (*Hamamelis vernalis*), 10

Pachysandra, 49–50
Paeonia suffruticosa (tree peony), 90, 91, 115, 116
pampas grass, 62
pansies, 66
parasitoids, 43
parterres, 13
partridge berry (*Mitchella repens*), 46–47
pathways, 18
Pattel, Rob, 59
pearlbush, 26
peat moss, 6
Penstemon, 28
peonies: in arrangements, 66; deer-resistance of, 25; and early plant explorers, 50; Japanese origins of, 91
perennials, tall native, 132–33
perovskias, 26, 67, 115
pesticides, 42, 48
pests, 46, 51
Philadelphus. See mock orange
Phlox subulata (Creeping phlox), 26, 29
photosynthesis, 40
Physocarpus. See ninebark
Picea glauca, 28, 37, 113
Pieris japonica. See Lily-of-the-Valley bush
pine, 69
Pinks (*Dianthus* spp.), 29
'Pink Storm' (*Chaenomeles*), 81
Pinus contorta 'Spaan's Dwarf', 28
'Pixie Dust' (*Picea glauca*), 28
Plant Hardiness Zone Map, 11, 136–37
planting shrubs, 5–6
plumbago, 22
poison sumac (*Toxicodendron*), 97
pollination and pollinators: agents of, 40–43; and biodiversity, 45; flowers' role in, 38; and hybrids, 39–40; and reproductive structures of flowers, 39
Possum-haw (*Viburnum nudum*), 79
predators, 34
'Prince Charles' (*Amelanchier*), 22
'Princess Diana' (*Amelanchier*), 22
privet, 14, 15, 115

promethea moth caterpillars, 46
pruning: in borders, 16–17; catching clippings, 21; of compact varieties, 3; espalier, 17; of flowering shrubs, 27; guidelines for, 35, 115; sub-shrubs, 12; topiaries, 17
prunus, 27, 68
pumilus (dwarf or low-growing) shrubs, 3
pussy willows, 62, 65
Pyracantha, 17, 116

Queen Anne's lace, 67
'Queen of the Night' tulips, 66

raspberries (*Rubus* genus): fruit of, 48, 52; and wildlife, 35, 52t
redbud trees, 62, 66
red chokeberries (*Aronia arbutifolia*), 52t, 82
'Red Imp' (*Hamamelis vernalis*), 25
red osier dogwoods (*Cornus sericea*), 86, 87
'Red Sprite' winterberry, 52, 111
repetition in garden design, 36, 113
reproductive function of flowers, 38–39
rhododendrons: in arrangements, 60, 67, 69; foliage of, 2, 9, 113; hybridization of, 50; and *Pieris japonica*, 77; requirements of, 25; *R. fortunei*, 50; sites for, 12; and wildlife, 34, 35
Rhus. See sumac
Ribes (gooseberries), 36, 52, 52t
roots, 5–6
rose mallow (*Hibiscus moscheutos*), 30
rosemary, 67
rose of Sharon (althea): 'Blue Bird', 31; in hedgerows, 37; self-sowing of, 3; sterile varieties of, 26; and wildlife, 53
roses (*rosa*): and alien pests, 51; fruit of, 52; invasive species of, 45; maintenance requirements of, 3–4; pruning of, 115; and wildlife, 35, 36, 52t
roughleaf dogwood (*Cornus drummondii*), 87
roundleaf dogwood (*Cornus rugosa*), 87
rove beetles, 43
royal fern (*Osmunda regalis*), 31
Rubus genus (blackberries/raspberries), 37, 52t
'Ruby Spice' (*Clethra alnifolia*), 103
Russian sage, 26, 115

Sackville-West, Vita, 25

sage: in arrangements, 66, 67, 68; Culinary sage (*Salvia officinalis*), 29, 115; in hedgerows, 37; pruning of, 115; Russian sage, 26, 115
Salvia officinalis (Culinary sage), 29, 115
Sambucus. See elderberries
sap-sucking emerald ash borers, 51
'Sarah' (*Kalmea latifolia*), 116
saucer magnolia tree, 62
scale considerations in plant selection, 18
seasons, 116; and appearance of shrubs, 8; and goal setting, 13; and wildlife, 37
sedges, 31
seed dissemination, 35
serviceberries (*Amelanchier*), 74, 75; *A. arborea*, 75; *A. humilis*, 75; *A. laevis*, 75; in arrangements, 66; 'Autumn Brilliance', 22; as foundational planting, 22; fruit of, 52; in hedgerows, 37; 'Prince Charles', 22; 'Princess Diana', 22; seasonal considerations for, 116; soil type requirements of, 6; and wildlife, 35, 36, 37, 52t
Shadbush. See serviceberries
shade-tolerant shrubs, 11, 123, 124
shape considerations in plant selection, 19
shining sumac (*Rhus copallina*), 97
shrub honey locust (*Gleditsia triacanthos* 'Elegantissima'), 27
shrubs, definition of, 2
'Sibirica' (*Cornus alba*), 116
silhouettes of plants, 8
silky dogwoods (*Cornus amomum*), 4, 86, 87
'Silver and Gold' (*Cornus sericea*), 87
sites for planting shrubs, 4–6, 29–32; evaluating property for, 12–13; exposure considerations, 12; and size of shrubs, 9; sloping sites, 12; and spacing considerations, 17–18
size of shrubs, 9
'Sky Pencil' (*Ilex crenata*), 36, 116
sloping sites, 12, 22, 26–27
Slow Flower movement, 60
small gardens, shrubs for, 117
smoke bush (*Cotinus*), 11, 17, 25
smooth sumac (*Rhus glabra*), 97
Snow Day (*Exochorda*), 26
snow drops, 4
'Snow Queen' (*Hydrangea quercifolia*), 28

soil, 43
'Somerset' daphne, 25
sourwood, 25
'Southern Belle' (hibiscus), 35
'Southern Gentleman' (winterberry),
   111
'Spaan's Dwarf' (*Pinus contorta*), 28
spacing shrubs, 17–18
spicebush (*L. benzoin*), 72, 73; in arrangements, 66; in hedgerows, 37;
   and insects, 45; shade-tolerance
   of, 11
spicebush swallowtails, 37, 45, 73
spireas, 119; in arrangements, 60, 62,
   65, 66, 67, 68; blooming habits of,
   23; 'Bridal Wreath', 66; in hedgerows, 37; *Spiraea × media*, 16t; *S.
   thunbergii*, 57; and wildlife, 35
spreading plants, 46–47
spruces: Alberta spruce, 113; in arrangements, 66, 67; blue spruce,
   66, 67, 112; and boxwoods, 48; and
   deer, 15; dwarf blue spruce, 48; foliage of, 9; and wildlife, 34, 37
'Squib' (*Hamamelis vernalis*), 25
staghorn sumac (*Rhus typhina*), 97
standards, 2
star magnolia (*Magnolia stellata*), 11
strawberry bush (*Calycanthus floridus*),
   100, 101
strawberry bush (*Euonymus americanus*), 53
subshrubs, 4, 12, 67, 115
suckers, 27
sumac (*Rhus aromatica*), 96, 97; in
   arrangements, 66; fruit of, 52;
   'Gro-Low' (*R. armoatica*), 97;
   in hedgerows, 37; poison sumac
   (*Toxicodendron*), 97; pruning of,
   115; smooth sumac (*R. glabra*), 97;
   staghorn sumac (*R. typhina*), 97;
   and wildlife, 35, 36, 46, 53; winged
   or shining sumac (*R. copallina*), 97
'Summer Snowflake' (*Viburnum plicatum*), 36, 79
summer sweet bush (*Clethra alnifolia*),
   102, 103; pruning of, 115; seasonal
   considerations for, 116
'Summer Wine' (*Physocarpus opulifolius*), 94
sun exposure, 5, 26–27
Swamp milkweed (*Asclepias incarnata*),
   31
sweet pepper bush (*Clethra*), 102, 103;
   pruning of, 115; seasonal considerations for, 116

Sweet Shrub (*Calycanthus floridus*),
   100, 101
Syringa. See lilacs

tags, nursery, 3, 5
Taxus canadensis, 37
Taxus cuspidata, 16t
tea, 50
Thuja orientalis (dwarf golden arborvitae), 113
topiaries, 17
'Toyo Nishiki' (*Chaenomeles speciosa*),
   27, 81
tree peony (*Paeonia suffruticosa*), 90,
   91, 115, 116
Tsuga, 16t, 28. See also hemlocks
tulips, 66
Turtlehead varieties, 31

Vaccinium. See blueberries
'Valley Rose' (*Pieris japonica*), 76
'Valley Valentine' (*Pieris japonica*), 77
'Vardar Valley' (*Buxus sempervirens*), 37
variety in the garden, 19–20
Vernonia fasciculata, 30
Vernonia gigantea, 30
viburnums (*Viburnum*): in arrangements, 60, 66, 68; Arrowwood
   (*V. dentatum*), 46, 79; black haw
   (*V. prunifolium*), 78, 79; 'Brandywine' (*V. nudum*), 79; 'Compacta'
   (*V. carlesii*), 79; and early plant
   explorers, 50; in hedgerows, 37;
   highbush cranberry (*V. trilobum*),
   37, 79; in mixed-shrub berms, 25;
   nannyberry (*V. lentago*), 79; Possum-haw (*V. nudum*), 79; pruning
   of, 115; seasonal considerations for,
   116; sites for, 15; 'Summer Snowflake' (*V. plicatum*), 36, 79; *V. acerifolium*, 11; and wildlife, 35, 36, 37,
   52t; 'Winterthur' (*V. nudum*), 11, 79
Victorian gardeners, 57
violas, 66
Virginia Sweetspire (*Itea virginica*), 99
Virginia witch-hazel, 57
vitex, 104, 105; 'Alba' (*V. agnus-castus*), 105; in arrangements, 62, 67;
   chaste tree (*V. agnus-castus*), 104,
   105; fiveleaf aralia (*V. Acanthopanax
   sieboldianus*), 16t; in island beds,
   23; 'Latifolia' (*V. agnus-castus*), 105;
   pruning of, 17, 115; sites for, 4

Wahoo (*Euonymus atropurpureus*),
   46, 53

walls in sunny sites, 26
Ward, Nathaniel, 50
wasps, 43
water for wildlife, 38, 43
watering guidelines, 6, 27–28, 35
water-witching, 109
weed prevention, 21
weeping blue juniper, 112
weeping willows, 62
weigelas: in arrangements, 67; blooming habits of, 17, 23; and early plant
   explorers, 50; pruning of, 115; and
   wildlife, 35, 53
wild hydrangea (*H. arborescens*), 11
wildlife, 34–53; benefits of shrubs for,
   2; and goal setting, 13; and native/
   nonnative shrubs, 10, 44–45, 48,
   128–29; as pollinators, 38; and seed
   dissemination, 35; water for, 38, 43
willows, 37, 115, 116
winged sumac (*Rhus copallina*), 97
winterberry (*Ilex verticillata*), 110, 111;
   in arrangements, 69, 111; fruit of,
   52, 111; 'Jim Dandy', 52, 111; in
   mixed-shrub berms, 52; 'Red Sprite',
   52, 111; seasonal considerations for,
   116; 'Southern Gentleman', 111;
   and wildlife, 46, 52t, 111; 'Winter
   Red', 111
wintercreeper vine, 45
'Winter Red' (winterberry), 111
'Winterthur' (*Viburnum nudum*), 11, 79
witch-alder, 125
witch-hazel (*Hamamelis*), 108, 109;
   'Arborea' (*H. japonica*), 25; 'Arnold
   Promise', 109; in arrangements, 60,
   63, 65; blooming habits of, 35; and
   boxwoods, 48; features of, 10; *H.
   mollis*, 25; *H. vernalis*, 4, 10, 25, 109;
   H. virginiana, 10, 35, 48, 108, 109;
   in mixed-shrub berms, 25; sites for,
   4; and wildlife, 35, 109
'Wolf Eyes' (*Cornus kousa*), 87
yarrow, 69
year-round color, 3
yews, 112; in arrangements, 65; in borders, 17; *Cephalotaxus harringtonia*
   (Japanese plum yew), 10; and deer,
   15; in hedgerows, 37; in hedges,
   13, 15; Japanese yews, 17; *Taxus
   canadensis*, 37; and wildlife, 34, 35

'Zebrina' (*Malva sylvestris*), 30
zinnia, 67

MOYA L. ANDREWS is Dean of the Faculties Emerita at Indiana University. A Master Gardener and author of numerous books, Andrews hosts *Focus on Flowers*, a weekly radio show on WFIU, an NPR affiliate, and writes gardening articles for *Bloom Magazine*. She is the author of *Perennials Short and Tall: A Seasonal Progression of Flowers for Your Garden* (IUP, 2008), which was illustrated by Gillian Harris.

Photo: Tom Stio, courtesy *Bloom Magazine*

GILLIAN HARRIS is a natural science illustrator and botanical artist. Her work has appeared in encyclopedias, field guides, museum and zoo displays, and international exhibits. She is an Indiana Master Naturalist and past president of the south-central chapter of the Indiana Native Plant and Wildflower Society (INPAWS), and she edits Indiana University Press's Indiana Natural Science series.

Photo: Will Cowan

EDITOR: *Linda Oblack*

PRODUCTION DIRECTOR: *Bernadette Zoss*

PROJECT EDITOR: *June Silay*

BOOK AND COVER DESIGN: *Pamela Rude*

PRINTER: *Oceanic Graphics*

Illustration on page ii: Ruby-throated hummingbird and New Jersey tea.

Library of Congress Cataloging-in-Publication Data

Andrews, Moya L.
Shrubs large and small : natives and ornamentals
for Midwest gardens / Moya L. Andrews and
Gillian Harris ; illustrated by Gillian Harris.
p. cm.
Natives and ornamentals for Midwest gardens
Includes bibliographical references and index.
ISBN 978-0-253-00906-7 (pbk. : alk. paper) —
ISBN 978-0-253-00914-2 (e-book)
1. Ornamental shrubs—Middle West. 2. Landscape
plants—Middle West. 3. Native plant gardening—
Middle West. I. Harris, Gillian, [date] II. Title.
III. Title: Natives and ornamentals for
Midwest gardens.
SB435.52.M5A53 2013
635.90977—dc23
2012034729